SCHNOOKS, CROOKS,
LIARS & SCOUNDRELS

SCHNOOKS, CROOKS, LIARS & SCOUNDRELS

A FIELD GUIDE TO IDENTIFYING POLITICAL BUFFOONS

GENE BERARDELLI

FOREWORD BY EVAN SAYET

ILLUSTRATIONS BY JOHN PENNISI

NEW DEGREE PRESS

COPYRIGHT © 2022 GENE BERARDELLI

All rights reserved.

SCHNOOKS, CROOKS, LIARS & SCOUNDRELS

A Field Guide to Identifying Political Buffoons

ISBN   979-8-88504-556-8   *Paperback*
            979-8-88504-882-8   *Kindle Ebook*
            979-8-88504-673-2   *Ebook*

For Dad, Grandpa, Grandma, and Aunt Barbara

CONTENTS

	FOREWORD BY EVAN SAYET	9
	A SATIRE, POINTED BY TRUTH	17

PART 1.   **THE LESSER HYPOCRITES**   **31**

CHAPTER 1. BLESS YOUR HEART:
              BUFFOONICUS SUPERSILLYOUS   33

CHAPTER 2. CHEWING UP THE SCENERY:
              BUFFOONICUS INCREDULOUS   45

CHAPTER 3. CHASING THE DRAGON:
              BUFFOONICUS CONTORTIUS   59

CHAPTER 4. LOST IN ALL THEIR GLORY:
              BUFFOONICUS OBLIVIOUS   75

PART 2.   **THE BÊTE NOIRE**   **93**

CHAPTER 5. SUCCUBI AND SNOLLYGOSTERS:
              BUFFOONICUS PARASITOS   95

CHAPTER 6. FOR THE CULTURE:
              BUFFOONICUS CELEBRITAS   107

CHAPTER 7. MERCENARY PENS AND MICS FOR HIRE:
              BUFFOONICUS AD-NEWSEAM   121

CHAPTER 8. PUSHING BEYOND THE ENVELOPE:
              BUFFOONICUS AMBITIOUS   137

PART 3.   **THE IRREDEEMABLES**   **149**

CHAPTER 9. THE TIPPING POINT:
              BUFFOONICUS SOPHISTRIUS   151

CHAPTER 10. TRIGGER WARNING:	
BUFFOONICUS EXTREMIS	167
CHAPTER 11. THE WRETCHED REFUSE:	
BUFFOONICUS DETESTICUS	181
SO... WHAT DID WE LEARN?	197
ACKNOWLEDGMENTS	215
APPENDIX	225

FOREWORD BY EVAN SAYET

It is always an honor when a friend and colleague asks you to write the foreword to their book. It means they believe that, out of all of the people in the world, it is you who possess a singular depth of knowledge about the subject at hand. When that subject is Buffoonery, it gives one pause.

While Gene makes light of fools in this book, I know from our ten-year friendship that he doesn't suffer them lightly, and thus I'm going to take the longevity of our association as evidence that my expertise in his eyes comes not from my possessing the traits of the Buffoon but rather from my having spent the whole of my adult life in close proximity to those who do.

Yeah, I'm going with that.

What would make Gene believe that I have had repeated intercourse with Buffoonery is that I spent the first half of my nearly forty-year career in Hollywood working with actors and the second half of my career in and around Washington working with politicians. The difference between the professions is simply this: The former are people whose job it is to pretend to be who they're not, while the latter's job is to pretend not to be who they are.

Hollywood and Washington may be on opposite coasts, but they are two sides of the same coin. And there's a *lot* of coin. So, it wasn't the least bit surprising to me to find many of the same characters—schnooks, crooks, liars, and scoundrels—in both professions.

Don't get me wrong. Not everyone in these industries falls into one of these categories. Far from it. There are, in fact, many good and decent people in the entertainment industry who wish for nothing more than to create moving works of great humanity. These people are kind and dedicated and can now be found working the counter at the Starbucks in Burbank. Similarly, there are many caring and decent people in politics who wish only to propose meaningful policy for the overall good. They're the ones manning the drive-thru at the McDonald's in Foggy Bottom.

The reality is that neither politics nor entertainment are populated with innately or inordinately bad people. It's that, for reasons discussed forthwith, neither of these industries tend to lend themselves to calls to the better angels or, perhaps better said, the better angels cannot always be heard above the din.

While Gene's book is an essential "how-to" (as in how to recognize the schnooks, crooks, liars, and scoundrels in politics),

I believe the service I can provide in these pages is to explain "why." What is it about the industries I've spent the whole of my adult life working in that might explain why they seem to be so disproportionately populated by Buffoons?

For one thing, both politics and the entertainment business are look-at-me industries. In these industries, the first thing a person must do is get people to look at them. Getting attention may not be the job's description, but it is how one gets to audition for the job. It's not a coincidence that "name recognition" is one of the best predictors of the outcome of an election, nor that an actor's "Q-Score" is one of the most successful indicators of a movie's eventual box office receipts. Buffoonery is just as good a means as any to garner attention in a field where being a stand-out guy comes before being a stand-up one.

It might be helpful, then, to think of politicians when they act and actors when they politick as being like one of those giant balloon-man thingies outside a car dealership. A lot of that handwaving and blowing in the wind is just to get you into the dealership.

What's different about the look-at-me industries is what they're trying to sell you once they've gotten you in the door. The car dealer tries to sell you a car. The lawn care provider tries to sell you his sodding and seeding services. If you're in the look-at-me industries, however, both the product and the services you're selling is *you*.

This makes for a great deal of conceit if for no other reason than that you're selling yourself at every moment. These other salespeople spend at least part of their day talking about something other than themselves. When what you're selling is *you* it's your job to talk about *you*. And, whereas the other salespeople close up shop and leave their products in the showroom, when you head home, you take your entire inventory—*you*—with you.

Everywhere you go, there *you* are. When you go out at night, there *you* are again. Everyone wants to meet *you* (but most people would be disappointed if they met you). It's worse than that, though; whereas the other salespeople only sell the product, you are the one who conceived of *you*, designed *you*, created *you*, manufactured, promoted, and distributed *you*, and you're continually updating *you*.

In fact, *you* are not just the product and the service; *you* are the company. Everyone who works for You, Inc. spends their day talking about *you*. *You* are what everyone around you spends their days conceiving, designing, constructing, manufacturing, promoting, selling, and distributing. When they write a press release, it's about *you*. When they appear on television it's to talk about *you* (but if they talk about you, *you* will fire them.)

It's even worse, still. Whereas other companies offer a whole line of products, You, Inc. sells only one product: *you*. The whole company rests on *you*. It lives and dies with *you*. The Ford Motor Company survived the Edsel because it had other cars to sell; Coca-Cola survived New Coke because they had other sodas to promote. At You, Inc., there's only *you*. As *you* go, so go you, *you*, and You, Inc., too.

At You, Inc. not only are you the only product, *you* have to make the sale. There is no second place in the look-at-me industries. Either you get the part, or you don't. Either you win the election, or you don't. In the *you* industry, there is no bragging, "We're number two, so we try harder"; there's only "We're number two. Would you like fries with that?"

Sure, not everyone in politics is running for elective office, but even in these other arenas, it's all about *you*. Al Sharpton (the quintessential Buffoon according to the rankings in this book) is the entire company selling just one product who desperately needs to call attention to himself at every turn. He needs to be not the winner of the election but chosen as *the* "voice" of his movement. Quick, name another "civil rights" spokesperson. Al Sharpton got the job.

It is the fact that there is no second place that makes winning paramount. Even if you're one of the good guys—and there are, in fact, many—who entered the profession to do good and to serve the public, all of it is meaningless if you don't win. There's a word for a good and righteous candidate who doesn't win. It's "loser."

Winning, then, becomes not just everything but the only thing. It's *righteous* to do what it takes to win because, if you don't, not only do you lose, not only do *you* lose, not only does everyone at You, Inc. lose, but, so, too, do the American people. That's what you—and everyone who works at You, Inc.—tell yourself. Because, if you don't win and bring your righteousness with you, then the schnook, crook, liar, and scoundrel who *isn't* righteous comes to power, and that wouldn't be good.

This is why it is helpful to think of politics like professional wrestling. Wouldn't you want Stone-Cold Steve Austin to bite a little when he's up against Jake "The Snake" Roberts? Doesn't he sort of have to? Wouldn't it be the *right* thing to do, or should he let the scoundrel win?

So, if politics is like professional wrestling, think of this book as the program. It's a way of keeping track of who's in the ring, who they're up against, and who the good guys and bad guys are. No one is pristine, and no one isn't a character. But there are people to root for and people to hiss at and people to cheer when they get hit over the head by a chair.

Gene's book is not only an essential who's-who, but it is also a timely one. It is needed now more than ever. While politics has always drawn a nefarious lot—just consider the Latin root of the word "politick": "poli" meaning "many" and "ticks" being blood-sucking insects—things are worse today than they've ever been, and this is not just me saying, "The kids these days." It would be hard to say such a thing when we're talking about a Speaker of the House who's in her eighties and a Senate majority leader fast approaching it.

What's changed isn't human nature; it's technology. Television, cable, and the Internet are the most recent technological changes to have done damage to our political system, but it was air conditioning that began its downfall.

For the first almost two hundred years of the republic, Washington wasn't just a metaphorical swamp; it was a literal one. It was dark and dank, musty and mosquito infested. It was like a Waffle House at 3 a.m. Nobody wanted to be there and, if you somehow found yourself there, you left as quickly as you sobered up.

With Washington now livable, people wanted to live there. They wanted to spend their lives there. They'd do whatever it took to get there and once there, they never wanted to leave. It is air conditioning that brought us the career politician, and it is the career politician who has brought us to where we are today. It changed who governed and why.

In days of yore, one made their fortune and then went into public service. Now people go into "public service" and then somehow go about making their fortunes. In fact, if they're really good, they somehow make their drug-addled son and ne'er-do-well in-laws' fortunes as well.

Politics as a career drew not the able but the ambitious. Whereas in days of old, elder statesmen arrived in Washington bringing with them a lifetime of experience, today a United States representative can arrive in Washington having never accomplished more than having kept her bar rag clean as she struggled to remember the recipe for a gin and tonic.

Compare and contrast, say, Ben Franklin, with the President of the United States, Joe Biden, who was first elected to the US Senate while still in his twenties and who is now so ossified that birds mistake him for a statue and poop on him. True story.

Franklin: Writer, scientist, inventor.

Biden:

Franklin: Statesman, diplomat, printer.

Biden:

Franklin: Publisher, philosopher, creator of the *Farmer's Almanac*.

Biden:

The advent of the career politician didn't just change Washington, it changed politics all up and down the line. Politics became a career with a career path. Washington thus grew in size and power. Local schnooks, crooks, liars, and scoundrels became *everyone*'s problem, television brought them into our homes, cable television did so on a 24/7 basis, and the Internet made them portable.

This is why, now more than ever, a way to keep track of just "who's who in Buffoonery" like this is so utterly essential and I can think of no better person to have written it. You know, because he's spent so much of his adult life surrounded by it.

Yeah, I'm going with that.

A SATIRE, POINTED BY TRUTH

We might as well begin at the beginning.

The word "Buffoon" can be traced back to the mid-sixteenth century when the term initially referred to professional comic actors, jesters, and fools (Harper, 2022). The English derived "buffoon" from the French *buffon* (Johnson, 1818), who, in turn, borrowed it from the Italian noun *buffone* (jester) as well as the verbs *buffa* (to jest) and *buffare* (to puff out the cheeks) (Harper, 2022). This latter derivation probably explains why a jester's head garment is known as a puffle cap, why "puffing" often refers to jesting, and "puffing up" has come to mean light exaggeration.

In the mid-eighteenth century, Samuel Johnson noted the expansion of the definition of "buffoon" thusly:

- A man whose profession is to make sport by low jests and antick postures; a jackpuddling.
- A man who practices indecent raillery.

Today's modern definition of "Buffoon" has been distilled further down to "one who sets himself to amuse by jests, grimaces, etc.; a low, vulgar or indecent jester, one without self-respect." (Leopold, 2021) That covers a whole lot of ground.

What you are about to explore is my belief that through the course of the evolution of American political culture, a multi-faceted definition specific to Political Buffoonery has emerged, with some politicians setting themselves to act as Buffoons intentionally as a tactic, and others to unintentionally become the subject of derision and ridicule out of sheer ignorance, hubris, or some combination thereof. How we get to that definition requires detailed observation of both American political history and modern political current events.

But first, a little personal history of how a few friendly chats over the past few years inspired this book.

THE ORIGINS OF THE TOTALLY MADE-UP PSEUDOSCIENCE OF "BUFFOONOLOGY"

In December of 2009, I was a wide-eyed optimist (or masochist, depending on your perspective) who wanted to help grow the Republican Party in what I have come to call "The People's Republic of New York." I was fresh off a rather dismal run for New York City Council as a Republican (Berke, 2009), and my experiences as a candidate left me somewhat disillusioned with the one-sided nature of my local politics. Merit meant nothing. These people would vote for a ham sandwich so long as it was registered Democrat.

So, with a run for office checked off my personal bucket list and the doldrums that come with being a Republican in one of the most liberal counties in the nation setting in, I needed to rediscover my joy for politics again. Thanks to three amazing friends, I did just that.

Mark Healey gave me the skills needed to find that joy. "Heals" is a true visionary who, unlike most of us, had the balls to follow his vision. Before I got into politics, I helped him start his own niche sports media brand hyper-focused on the past, present, and future of New York baseball called Gotham Baseball. (Healey, 2020) One of Mark's more brilliant ideas was developing what I believe was the first on-location live sports podcast, which originated from Mickey Mantle's restaurant in Manhattan. (Ibid.) Mark was the talent, and he asked if I could run the technical end; at Gotham, everyone wore multiple hats, and it was always "all hands on deck." The fun I had with Heals putting on that show got me thinking that I could replicate my own niche show but with local politics, in a concept I called *Brooklyn GOP Radio*.

Craig Eaton gave me the means to pursue that joy. In addition to being one of my political mentors, Craig was the Chairman of the local Republican Committee. In January of 2010, I pitched *Brooklyn GOP Radio* as a means to draw in younger volunteers so we could counter well-funded Democrat candidates. Thankfully, he greenlit the project, gave me a small budget for equipment, and allowed me to use the county office as a base of operations. I was off to the races.

Russell Gallo provided the fire that reignited my joy again. Russ was a colleague who regularly attended the same local meetings I did. It was hard not to spot us; we were usually the only thirty-somethings among rooms full of geriatrics. So, we naturally gravitated toward each other. His outspoken and fearless manner was made for a project like *Brooklyn GOP Radio*. Thankfully, it only took one show recorded at my house to get him hooked on the idea, and our on-air chemistry and personal friendship grew from there. Now, *we* were off to the races.

Within a year, thanks to a combination of my new platform and Russ's talent for organization, *Brooklyn GOP Radio* found over one hundred new campaign volunteers, many of whom became dear friends I keep to this day. Incredibly, those volunteers we found helped deliver election victories for Republicans running in Brooklyn of all places! Chairman Eaton gave credit to Russ, me, and our show for our small roles in a Brooklyn GOP "Renaissance" (Benjamin, 2012). We even created an award-winning new Young Republicans club by using the show. Every Wednesday night became an impromptu party night. Anywhere from ten to twenty of us would meet up at the office, order some pizzas from next door, talk about the politics of the day on air, and end up at a bar in the Bay Ridge neighborhood of Brooklyn.

We expanded our horizons outside of our Brooklyn bubble by traveling to national conservative conventions and began discussing more national politics. With Chairman Eaton's blessing, Russ and I rebranded *Brooklyn GOP Radio* to reflect the national following we were earning (Witt, 2015), and *Behind Enemy Lines Radio* was born. Long story short, Russ and I syndicated our little show into a terrestrial radio show (Talkers, 2015) broadcast in multiple states, we won a hotly contested national award (Hughes, 2015), we threw a legendary party involving a congressman and a hot tub that made national news (Heil, 2015), and we even had a semi-weekly national column (Newsmax, 2022). It was quite the ride for many years.

But most relevant to this discussion, the focus of both *Brooklyn GOP Radio* and *Behind Enemy Lines Radio* turned to analyzing the missteps of many politicians. Themes like political hypocrisy and pointing out downright foolish behavior cropped up so much in our discussions, that Russell and I created a segment called "Buffoon of the Week" where we debated which newsmaker in politics was the biggest Buffoon. Needless to say, we found no shortage of potential nominees. This, in turn, culminated annually into a "Buffoon of the Year" tournament where listeners could debate and choose the dumbest newsmaker of the year.

The debates comparing various political Buffoons had a happy ferocity to them, which helped us communicate to the audience not only why what we observed was so hilarious, but also pointed out lessons learned through dissecting our observations. We took Buffoonery seriously, and our audience ate it up. The segment's popularity snowballed into a fun sociological experiment.

BUNS AND BAMS: CREATING THE SHARPTON BUFFOONERY MATRIX™
What follows is the culmination of over a decade of happy debates, arguments, and discussions between me and any combination of my closest friends Russell Gallo, Diana Gallo,

Amanda Kohut, and especially, Matthew Fairley, who singlehandedly devised the framework I am about to outline.

When we started *really* calling out Political Buffoonery, our discussions boiled down to a common agreement that we knew it when you saw it. "Buffoonology" was so primitive because society had failed to establish even the most rudimentary tools, like basic units of measurement or even a common lexicon. Out of our friendly interactions, we created our own shorthand to better identify and describe the Political Buffoonery occurring all around us all the time.

To start, we needed a common understanding of scale that would allow us to communicate to a lay person the significance of the observed Buffoon or Buffoonish act (Fairley, 2015). So, our first goal was to create an agreeable reference for measuring the dual aspects of Political Buffoonery: one's personal Buffoonish Nature (BUN) and the Buffoonish Action Magnitude (BAM) of one's Buffoonish acts.

Let's talk BUNs. A decade of collective observations has shown that everyone, to some degree, has a BUN. You. Me. Everyone. But, to paraphrase Orwell in *Animal Farm*, all Buffoons are created equal, but some Buffoons are more equal than others. The size of our BUNs is directly related to one's propensity to commit a Buffoonish act. If you doubt this, you needn't look further than our political class in America. As Thomas Paine once said, "The trade of governing has always been monopolized by the most ignorant and the most rascally individuals of mankind" (Bennett, 1925).

Politics contains not only a disproportionate number of Buffoons within it as compared to society in general, but a politician's BUN is decidedly bigger and more prominently displayed than your average Joe. This makes Political Buffoonery fertile ground for field study.

We answered the need for a BUN-measuring tool by establishing The BUN Scale™, a finite rating system from zero to one hundred, which allows us to compare each politicians' BUNs and come to an agreement on who is the bigger Political Buffoon.

The only remaining problem was identifying a lodestar—someone we can unanimously agree possesses the biggest BUN of all. Thankfully, as I will discuss extensively throughout, the good Lord gave us a walking, unintelligibly talking, track-suited, chain-wearing frame of reference in the Rev. Al Sharpton. Rev. Al's decades-long adventures in Buffoonery are legendary, as you will see herein. His selection, of course, was unanimous, establishing him as the only (as yet known) perfect hundred on The BUN Scale™.

As for the bottom of The BUN Scale™, one would find those perfect individuals whose every action is widely considered pure and noble, such as Jesus, Buddha, Gandhi, or Weird Al Yankovic. Anyone will do, as we will spend very little time on the lower end of The BUN Scale™.

Having established that everybody falls somewhere within The BUN Scale™, and that one's overall propensity for committing acts of Buffoonery determines the size of your BUN, we moved on to establishing a means for measuring acts of

Buffoonery. The simple answer was to base the size of one's BUN on the magnitude of past acts of Buffoonery, which we call BAM. Each observed Buffoonish act needs an agreed-upon BAM score, which we can then plot along a second scale that has no defined upper limit. Like BUNs, an act's BAM is ranked in comparison to other acts.

To quantify the comparisons, we need another standard unit of measurement. Once again, drawing inspiration from our perfect Buffoon, the Rev. Al, we created "The Sharpton™." We established some concept of scale for "The Sharpton™" through a series of contextual examples, with acts of greater significance rating higher.

Private Buffoonish acts have a low BAM. For example, locking your keys in your car would come in somewhere around fifty Sharptons™, while forgetting your anniversary is clearly a higher magnitude in comparison, and would score around the range of seventeen KiloSharptons™.

Public displays of Buffoonery have a higher BAM because of its greater impact on society and culture. For example, NASA losing a Mars space probe because the engineering team used inches in their calculations but the flight team used centimeters (Lloyd, 1999) has to be somewhere in the hundreds of MegaSharptons™ range. Even bigger actions, like President Bill Clinton asking "what the meaning of the word 'is' is" while giving testimony before a grand jury, gets up into the rarified air of GigaSharptons™.

Measuring BAM for each action seems straightforward enough. But this concept gets trickier when trying to determine the relationship between the BAM of a Buffoon's action and his/her BUN. Thus, the Sharpton Buffoonery Matrix™ was born (Fairley, 2015).

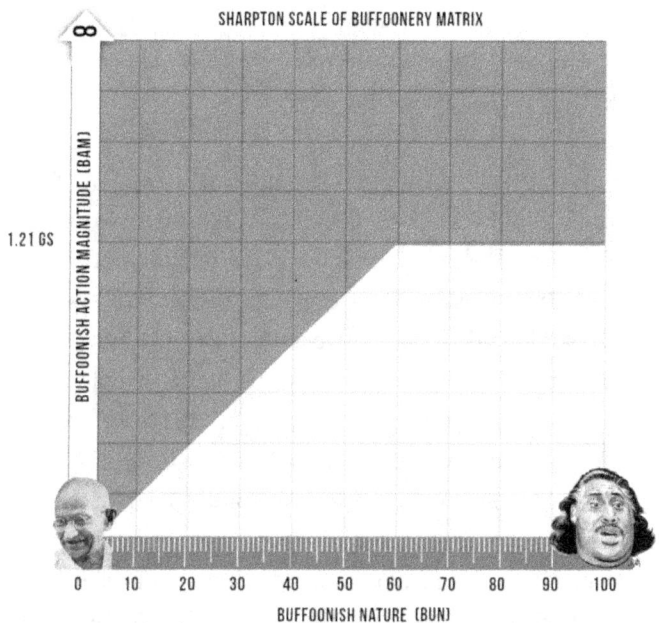

In general, the greater an action's BAM, the more likely one's BUN increases. Buffoons with lower BUN scores are more likely to see their BUN grow if she/he commits an act with an inordinately high BAM, while Buffoons with already large BUNs need to commit an act with a real doozy of a BAM to see any upward BUN movement. Thus, moving into to the upper echelons of Buffoonery requires acts of higher and higher BAM as your BUN score increases.

That sliding scale gives way when one's BUN gets higher than sixty. At that point, we draw a line in the sand and declare that only Buffoonish acts with a BAM reaching into the GigaSharptons™ will trigger an increase in BUN. But where should we draw that line? For this, we take inspiration from noted genius, Dr. Emmet Brown (Futurepedia, 2022) and declare that an act with a BAM of 1.21 GigaSharptons™ and above always triggers an increase in BUN. Those acts are collectively identified as Sharpton-esque.

As you can imagine, different permutations arise when analyzing a Buffoon's BUN-to-BAM ratio. It is possible for one's BUN to be and remain high even if she/he does not commit frequent Buffoonish acts, so long with his/her average BAM score is sufficiently high. Conversely, one can be prone to act Buffoonishly more frequently, but if his/her average BAM score is mild or moderate, that person's BUN will remain smaller. A good example of this is President George W. Bush. During his presidency, Dubya was prone to near-daily malapropisms, but each crime against the English language carried a low BAM, which, in turn, did not cause any significant increase in his BUN. Knowing one's BUN-to-BAM ratio is also useful in differentiating between a benign Buffoon whose average BAM is usually low, and an irredeemable with a high average BAM.

These tools represent a good first step, but Buffoonery remains unpredictable. At all times, someone who possesses lower BUNs remains just as susceptible to committing Sharpton-esque acts as Buffoons with big BUNs. Hopefully, by using our newly developed tools and through constant observation, we can fully identify those Buffoons already in office and marginalize their impact on society.

THE CHALLENGE OF OUR TIME: UNDERSTANDING POLITICALLY BUFFOONISH BEHAVIOR

While exposing known Buffoons and quantifying their societal impact are important, we need to identify future Buffoons faster. Like storm chasers in the Midwest looking to predict the next F5 faster to minimize loss of life, we too must strive to recognize predictive behavior before we have a full-blown Buffoon on our hands, and, maybe, prevent the next would-be dumbass Buffoon from taking office.

One can only dream of such a day.

Therefore, it is imperative to understand what makes a political Buffoon tick. As you will see, classifying a single Buffoonish act will be relatively easy and only requires good common sense and a keen eye to connect a Buffoon's personality to his/her resultant act. Consider these questions:

- What is it within the character of a person that causes him/her to act like a Buffoon?
- What traits are indicators of the Buffoonish behavior we should expect from a given Buffoon?
- Why do some Buffoons repeat the same kind of behavior as other deposed Buffoons?
- Why do some Buffoons transition into greater destructive behavior?
- How and why most Buffoons are "mutts," or hybrids possessing a dominant set of traits and one or more secondary traits of multiple Buffoon classifications within their nature?
- Can we predict future Buffoonery based on past Buffoonish acts?

To attempt to answer these questions, this book will act as a field guide classifying Buffoonish people and actions already observed in the wild. Each chapter will present a discrete Buffoon classification complete with a discussion of known traits and characteristics generally common within the classification and presentation of case studies from both history and modern-day news and current events to flesh out the recognition of the classification's characteristics and traits. These classifications range from silly to serious to even dark. Each chapter will also include a brief example of how our perfect Buffoon, Rev. Al Sharpton, fits into each classification I identify.

HOW TO REALLY USE THIS BOOK
To be clear, while this work is intended to make you laugh a little (I mean, c'mon. BUNs and BAMs?) it is also intended to provoke thought about the character, or lack thereof, within our political leaders going back to the birth of our great nation. As President John Quincy Adams once wrote, "The sting of Satire is never so sharp, as when pointed by truth."

As we prepare to take a deep dive into Political Buffoonery, please know there is no right or wrong way to read this book. If you prefer to read straight through from cover to cover, then be my guest. If one classification piques your interest more than others, then by all means, pick and choose what you like.

However you choose to read this book, keep in mind that our pseudoscience of Buffoonology is never settled. So please feel free to "get your hands dirty" and use this humble presentation as a jumping-off point for making your own observations. I am not so arrogant to say that I know all there is to know about Political Buffoonery, so I welcome—and encourage—you to share your thoughts with me and with others. Together, we can better understand Political Buffoonery and, one day, stamp it out of existence.

PART I

THE LESSER HYPOCRITES

CHAPTER 1

BLESS YOUR HEART: BUFFOONICUS SUPERSILLYOUS

In politics, as in life, you are bound to encounter characters who, either intentionally or unconsciously, say or do things so hilariously Buffoonish that the only rational response is a shake of the head or a laugh proportional to the Buffoonish magnitude of the action. Such is the reaction elicited by *Buffoonicus supersillyous,* commonly known as...

THE "BS" BUFFOON
For the average person, our inner "BS" Buffoon emerges in isolated moments known as, what we in pseudoscientific circles call, *cerebellum flatulus,* commonly known as "brain farts." Given the common nature of the occurrence, little need be said on these tendencies, as we all can relate to the feelings when these momentary lapses happen.

For the politically active, the dominant characteristic of this rather common and typically harmless Buffoon is an overabundance of self-confidence that masks a deficiency in their nature or ability, which ultimately becomes their undoing. In many ways, the "BS" Buffoon is reminiscent of a young child who knows without a doubt they can reach that top shelf or turn a cartwheel on their first try. The attempt often ends in a charming failure that all involved can laugh off as a learning experience. But while the child learns from failure, the "BS" Buffoon rarely does.

Thus, more often than not, the "BS" Buffoon's inner deficiency is ignorance. The "BS" Buffoon is typically so self-assured in their assumed knowledge or expertise on any given topic, but in actuality, the "BS" Buffoon stands at a distinct disadvantage in comparison to a *bona fide* expert. Moreover, their self-confidence mixed with ambition overwhelms their reason to such an extent that "BS" Buffoons will often hold their rhetorical ground even the face of contrary *bona fide* expertise. When confronted with their own intellectual failings, many "BS" Buffoons will "double down" until they are roundly shamed. The more recalcitrant "BS" Buffoons will cling to their positions, armed with the foolhardy belief that they cannot be wrong and therefore, the world must be wrong.

Alternatively, their deficiency comes from their lack of skill. "BS" Buffoons often find themselves in a position where their reach exceeds their grasp. They often fail to rise to the occasion, no matter how large or small. Whether it be the bright lights of a camera, the sight of scrolling text on the teleprompter, or the stares of a gathering crowd hanging on their every word, the "BS" Buffoon is sure to stammer, stumble, flub, or flop at a crucial moment.

Do not confuse "BS" Buffoons with other Buffoons discussed later herein. For example, a "BS" Buffoon may try to bend known facts adverse to its position to fit them into their point of view much like *Buffoonicus contortius,* also known as the Agenda Gymnast. Also, "BS" Buffoons often fail to realize that their personal deficiency has been fully exposed, much like the Political Narcissist, *Buffoonicus oblivious.* Thus, each person's Buffoonish nature is a unique hybrid combination.

Buffoonicus supersillyous should not be confused with its less endearing cousin, *Buffoonicus sophistrius*—the Hypocrite—who bears some similarities, but with an air of malignant arrogance. Remember, the "BS" Buffoon is, typically, not a bad actor—just a misguided one. She/He is often well-meaning or blissfully naive. They simply do not know any better, and thus, one cannot ascribe malintent to their activities. That said, it is rather common for a "B.S" Buffoon to "graduate" into the Hypocrite, depending on the hybrid makeup of one's Buffoonish nature after suffering the mounting frustration associated with one or multiple publicly embarrassing or shameful moments. In this respect, the "BS" Buffoon operates as sort of a jumping-off point to deeper and darker levels of Buffoonery.

THE BUFFOONISH ORIGINS OF AN AMERICANISM
The story of Congressman Felix Walker of Buncombe County, North Carolina, presents what many may point to as a seminal moment of American Buffoonery.

For our purposes, the relevant portion of Walker's life that merits our examination occurred while he was a member of the sixteenth Congress.[1] The date is February 25, 1820, and Walker rises on the floor of the House of Representatives to address the question of admitting the territory of Missouri to the Union (Annals of Congress, 1820). This was a particularly weighty topic was before Congress because the question of western expansion was inextricably intertwined with the abhorrent practice of slavery.

The delicate balance of parity was about to shift; the then-twenty-two states were split down the middle, with Missouri primed to upset that balance. Walker was steeping into a corrosive debate over allowing western states to continue practicing America's "original sin" at a time that history would recall as the Missouri Compromise. Surely, Walker must have planned a great oratory to put his contemporaries to shame and thus leave his mark on history for contributing to a pivotal debate—which, as many historians note, was a tipping point for a young America.

Well, Walker indeed left a mark in *The Annals of Congress*. But I would not exactly say that he rose to the occasion:

> *Mr. WALKER, of North Carolina, rose then to address the Committee on the question; but the question was called for so clamorously and so perseveringly that Mr.*

---

[1] The author notes that, if you have the time or the inclination, it is well worth the effort to examine Mr. Walker's life and times as a soldier, politician, and pioneer, as he is a man who experienced both the opportunities and opportunism of early America that most have likely not have read about in your high school history books.

> *W. could proceed no farther than to move the Committee Rise.*
>
> *The Committee refused to rise, by almost a unanimous vote.*

(Annals of Congress, 1820). Historical accounts of the time note that Walker's speech was long, dull, and irrelevant (Safire, 2008) to the momentous vote to come. One account notes that other members of Congress interrupted the tedious Walker, telling him it was no use to go on, while other members left (Bartlett, 2003).

Defeated and out of his depth, Walker is said to have uttered, "Never mind; I was talking for Buncombe" (Ibid.).

And with that turn of phrase, Walker had memorialized a deliciously colorful term that would forever become associated with useless political claptrap that Buffoons espouse: Buncombe. This true Americanism's etymology has since morphed through time into the word "bunkum," (Ibid.) and then, eventually, "bunk" (Safire, 2008).

Felix Walker is the embodiment of a "BS" Buffoon making history for all the wrong reasons. While it is true that what has since been defined as "bunk" existed long before Walker was "speaking to Buncombe," it took a vacuous speech within the chamber of the House of Representatives for a truly American practice to be exquisitely defined. In essence, Walker has become a founding father of American Buffoonery. The dissemination of "bunk" by Buffoonish politicians walking in this pioneer's footsteps has grown exponentially and in proportion with the development and expansion of means of communication. What started in scant accounts in newspapers and pamphlets has grown to include direct mailings, automated telephone calls, broadcast interviews in both audio and video formats, emails, SMS and direct messaging, online social media postings, and other calls to action seeking money and votes. Today, every politician at all levels is "talking for Buncombe"; in fact, today's members of Congress are never not "talking for Buncombe," as every word travels at the speed of light within a twenty-four-hour news cycle with the hope of striking the right chord with their targeted audience.

While Walker may have coined the phrase, many generations have gone on to perfect the practice.

THE GENTLEMAN FROM GEORGIA'S PROCLIVITY TO INSERT FOOT DIRECTLY INTO MOUTH

Perhaps no modern "BS" Buffoon can better compare to Walker than the rhetorical adventures of Rep. Hank Johnson (D-GA). His manner has been described as a "slow, almost confused drawl" that "punctuates comments that are often ripe for conservative ridicule" (Fuller, 2013).

Absent from Johnson's self-created list of accomplishments (Johnson, 2013) is his most public display that occurred during a full committee hearing of the House Armed Services Committee held on March 25, 2010. The hearing concerned allocation of defense funds as part of the 2011 National Defense Authorization Act (NDAA) (GovInfo, 2010). The business of the day was to conduct a "posture hearing," involving senior civilian and military leadership of the US Department of Defense, the military services, and other certain defense agencies invited to testify before the committee on particular budget requests associated with the NDAA (Heitshusen, et. al., 2020). During this hearing, Johnson pursued a bizarre line of questioning that many still talk about to this day concerning a proposed increased allocation of military personnel on the small Micronesian island of Guam (Ibid.). But that story's been told to death.

Another glowing, albeit lesser known, Buffoonish moment in Johnson's career stemmed from his admitted tendency to analogize in his speeches à *la* eccentric billionaire-turned-presidential-candidate H. Ross Perot, who was also famously lampooned for his use of analogies out of left field (NBC, 2016). But unlike the folksy and endearing Perot, the congressman who thought an island would tip over would not fare so well.

On December 12, 2012, Johnson addressed the whole of Congress about his concerns over a new right-to-work law in Michigan brought by Republicans. Johnson saw the law as an affront to the National Labor Relations Act, (Rojas, 2012), likening the struggle of labor and management to a WWE cage fight between giants and little people. "I was thinking to myself earlier today, what happens when you put in a cage fight a giant with a midget?" Johnson said. "Well, the midget will not win the fight. I'm going to tell you that. Why? He just doesn't carry enough weight to do so. But if you put thirty midgets in with that giant, then the midgets have a chance" (Kim, 2012).

Apparently, in Johnson's zeal to show his rudimentary knowledge of why workers unionize, he had stumbled into an offensive term. According to the *Associated Press Stylebook*, the term "midget," though used in the past to describe an unusually short and proportionate person, is widely considered derogatory. Indeed, a term like "little people" had been in common use for some time (National Center on Disability and Journalism, 2018).

The next day, Johnson shared with the House like a recovering alcoholic uses an AA meeting:

> As I am prone to do, I use a lot of analogies, and so last night I used an analogy that some find offensive. And I certainly was not meaning to be offensive or use a derogatory term. Everybody knows what the N-word is.
>
> I had never heard of the M-word…. The M-word is a word also that describes a group of people. It, at

one time, had been commonly used as a descriptive term. It was, at one time, socially acceptable. But to my discovery, just within the last twelve hours or so, I have found that the use of the M-word is no longer socially acceptable.

Now, the M-word refers to a group of people, the little people.... It really refers to a medical condition. "Dwarfism" is the name of that medical condition. And sometimes I guess one can even say "abnormally small people." I like that term better than "dwarfism."

So, I wanted to say to all of those who may have been offended by my use of the M-word, I want you to know that it was out of ignorance and not spite or hatred that I used that term. And please know that I will never use that term again.

(House of Representatives, 2012). Johnson's "learning moment" became fodder for tabloids and social media users (Twitchy, 2012). Some decried the age of political correctness, while others poked fun at Johnson turning the floor of the most powerful legislative body in the world into this own personal support group.

And while it did not make it into the refined record of the Caucus meeting, I note that Johnson did indeed slip and use the "M-word" again during a speech where he vowed to never use that word again (Schneier, 2012). Old Buffoonish habits die hard, I guess.

But, beyond the use of the "M-word," Johnson still stood behind the substance of what he said because, "even though it used the wrong wording, [it] was a great analogy in my personal opinion" (House of Representatives, 2012).

And there, dear readers, you have the hubris of the unrepentant "BS" Buffoon.

The Shakespearian phrase "jack of all trades, master of none" comes to mind when thinking of the many hats worn by our Perfect Buffoon. Here, we focus on Rev. Al, the television host.

With no media background other than the fact that he has been a frequent blowhard on our airwaves for decades, Rev. Al signed a deal for his own *MSNBC* "politi-tainment" show called *PoliticsNation* on August 29, 2011 (Stelter, 2011).

Since then, Rev. Al has been the gift that keeps on giving. His frequent flubs, miscues, delays, and misstatements, many of which are cataloged on social media, have generated millions of online views and just as many laughs. Sharpton regularly massacres names and common everyday words alike as they roll across his teleprompter. Among such memorable Sharpton mis-phrases are:

- "Resist we much" (Washington Free Beacon, May 6, 2014);
- "Thigh military" (Washington Free Beacon, May 17, 2014); and
- "UseTube celebrities" (Washington Free Beacon, Jan. 26, 2015).

The man was and is, clearly, out of his depth.

Sadly, those heady days may now be behind us, as Sharpton's ratings dropped so low that *MSNBC* removed Rev. Al from his plum weekday prime time slot and relegated him to the weekends in September 2015 (Steinberg, 2015).

CHAPTER 2

CHEWING UP THE SCENERY: BUFFOONICUS INCREDULOUS

Any astute observer of politics will tell you that another fairly common indication you are dealing with a Buffoon is an extreme emotional response to current events. I am sure you can conjure the image of those screaming snowflakes who completely lost their minds when President Donald Trump was inaugurated. I would wager that you can picture the memes as you read this: the wailing, the crying, the uncontrolled fits of anger.

For me, I immediately flash back to a time when I was still involved in institutional politics on the local level: an "insurgency" attempted to take over the leadership of the local county party, of which I was a part. Long story short: They failed in court (Schmidt, 2014). But, on the day of our courtroom victory, a rogue member of our county committee named Glenn Nocera, a political gadfly who once referred to my political mentor Craig Eaton as a "nasty son of a bitch"

(Bredderman, 2013) in an open meeting, locked the county leadership out of its own Facebook page and deleted any post mentioning his faction's epic loss.[2] It was maybe the most childish thing I've even seen a middle-aged man do without the benefit of intoxication.

Episodes like this remind me how lucky I was to leave that fishbowl of local institutional politics on my own terms with my sanity and dignity intact. The misadventures of Glenn and many other experiences got me thinking specifically about all the political hysterics that stem from uncontrolled emotions.

New York Times best-selling author and Pulitzer Prize winner Charles Duhigg, having spoken with James Averill, professor emeritus of psychology at the University of Massachusetts, Amherst, once wrote in *The Atlantic:*

> *Anger… is one of the densest forms of communication. It conveys more information, more quickly, than almost any other type of emotion. And it does an excellent job of forcing us to listen to and confront problems we might otherwise avoid.*

---

[2] A brief note on Glenn: The years of comedy generated from watching his antics over the years brought so much joy to the lives of my friends and me that it influenced our advancements in our pseudoscience of Buffoonology. One could say he was the first Buffoon we truly studied up close in his natural habitat. And what a body of work there was to study! So cheers, Glenn. Your curious political decision-making may not have only earned you much in ways of notoriety or respect (a clear message drawn from that 7 percent you "earned" in that 2008 election), but consider your immortalization in this book as the original "Hot Mess" proof of a well-earned "legacy."

Wise words, but I fear the definition falls apart when politics is involved. Using Professor Averill's learned statement as sort of a guiding theme, we are ready to examine *Buffoonicus incredulous*, colloquially known as...

THE HOT MESS

The dominant characteristic of the Hot Mess is a proclivity to fall into fits of emotional turmoil in moments of great political stress. That is because the Hot Mess has little rational or intellectual discourse to offer and is left with no other avenue than to appeal to emotion during these peak moments of stress. For example, you are sure to encounter a Hot Mess in the waning weeks of a hotly contested campaign or during some other highly scrutinized political event or occasion, like a march, a protest, or a hearing. The higher the stress level, the more likely you are to observe the Hot Mess even spew a few personal attacks or pitiful outbursts—especially when things aren't going their way. As you'll see, the Hot Mess is one of many Buffoons who act as a gateway to Buffoons with typically higher BAM on average, which we categorize as "Irredeemable."

The Hot Mess proves Prof. Averill is absolutely correct in noting that the speed of information increases during an angry emotional eruption, but I fear his latter statement is incorrect. As the Hot Mess approaches terminal velocity of thought, she/he sacrifices clarity and logic in favor of an uncontrolled stream-of-consciousness diatribe that devolves the discourse into unredeemable absurdity. Remember, the Hot Mess's personal emotional spectrum is wide and freewheeling. A Hot Mess may exhibit uncontrollable happiness or an improper affect to a given situation and can "run hot and cold" at even a moment's notice.

Take, for instance, Vice President Kamala Harris's inappropriate laughter when confronted with questions about the 2021 border crisis (Salo, et. al., 2021). Harris reacted similarly when confronted about the Biden administration's disastrous withdrawal from Afghanistan (Brown, 2021). It seems to be her thing. One would be forgiven for likening Vice President Harris's reactions to Joaquin Phoenix's portrayal of pseudobulbar affect (PBA), (Mayo Clinic, 2018), the sudden controllable and inappropriate laughing or crying of the brain-damaged psychopath in *Joker* (Groth, 2019).

While I am by no means versed in psychology or any medical field whatsoever, it would not be unreasonable to hypothesize that the Hot Mess has issues bubbling under the service of their otherwise polished political persona. However, science has yet to uncover a correlation between heated political outbursts and being certifiably cuckoo bananas—though an hour on Facebook might change your mind.

Ultimately, the Hot Mess overshadows the issue and nothing gets done. Their machinations and incoherence emphasize their personal fragility over the importance of the position they advocated. Depending upon the perceived level of the outburst, reactions to a Hot Mess range from laughter to uneasiness to dismissal as a craven lunatic.

There is another tactic that a Hot Mess uses that is arguably more devious. Knowing the power that emotion carries, the Hot Mess will try manipulating the emotions of others. In these instances, the Hot Mess puts up the *appearance* of an emotional display as a way to enflame his/her audience's emotional state. Some would recognize this as the acts of a "drama queen" craving attention and support, but with a deeper ulterior political motive reminiscent of *Buffoonicus sophistrius*, the Hypocrite.

Regardless of tactics, the Hot Mess thrives on creating and exposing other Hot Messes. But like *Buffoonicus contortius*, which we will examine later, the Hot Mess eventually runs out of the currency of personal credibility each time she/he keeps going back to that emotional well. And, with each successive act of emotional desperation, both BUN and BAM grow.

THE FIRST "HOT MESS" PRESIDENT

Hot Messes engross themselves in self-inflicted drama like settling scores and one-upping a rival. Some of the greatest men of our history, our Founding Fathers, were not immune to overblown displays of emotion. Perhaps the angriest of them all was our second President, John Adams, who regularly fell prey to his own anger. As Alexander Hamilton describes in correspondence from 1800:

> It is a fact that [President Adams] is often liable to paroxisms of anger, which deprive him of self command, and produce very outrageous behaviour to those who approach him. Most, if not all his Ministers, and several distinguished Members of the two Houses of Congress, have been humiliated by the effects of these gusts of passion.

Neither Adams nor Hamilton had a flattering opinion of the other. Adams, on more than one occasion, referred to Hamilton as "a bastard brat of a Scotch Pedler" (Adams, 1806). Adams's pimp hand was strong. He even called George Washington "Old Muttonhead" (Smith, 1994) in one of his crankier moments!

But let's turn to a more concrete and well-reported instance of Adams's famed temper. Fresh off the diplomatic dust-up of the XYZ Affair and the Quasi-War (US State Dept., 2021) with France in 1799, Adams dispatched diplomats to negotiate a new treaty with the French without consulting his Secretary of War James McHenry or his Secretary of the Treasury Oliver Wolcott (Hamilton, 1799)—both of whom were loyal to his political rival, that "bastard brat" Hamilton (McHenry, May 31, 1800).[3]

Hamilton would later meet with Adams in Trenton to dissuade him from his intended course, a move that Adams saw as a set-up by his "disjointed" cabinet (McHenry, May 20, 1800). McHenry would later write about Adams angrily confronting him about Hamilton's unexpected appearance, quoting Adams:

> You are subservient to Hamilton, who ruled Washington, and would still rule if he could. Washington saddled me with three Secretaries who would controul me, but I shall take care of that. [W]hat do any of you know

---

[3] If you're into the history of early American foreign policy, look it up on your own, you nerd... We've got serious Buffoonery to discuss!

of the diplomatic Interests of Europe? You are all mere children who can give no assistance in such matters.

How could such men presume to advise in such matters, or dare to recommend a suspension of the Mission to France. You too joined in the Advice, and are too subservient to Wolcott and [Secretary of State Timothy] Pickering.

(McHenry, May 31, 1800). And you thought that presidential belligerence was a modern invention?

McHenry would later write that "[a]t times he would speak in such a manner of certain men and things, as to persuade one that he was actually insane" (McHenry, May 20, 1800).

Adams's anger and paranoia were borne from the pressures of the election politics of his time. McHenry believed that "the acts of administration were, as far as practicable to be made subservient to electioneering purposes" (Ibid.) and that "[e]very day increased his alarm... and distrust of those gentlemen... who did not constantly feed him with news or hopes flattering to his election." (Ibid.) And he was probably right. But just because Adams let his paranoia fuel his anger doesn't mean he was wrong in thinking that everyone was out to get him. As history recounts, the election of 1800 was one of the most bitterly contested in our history, with Adams narrowly losing to Thomas Jefferson.

SENATOR SPARTACUS'S SOUND AND FURY SIGNIFYING BUFFOONERY

When talking about political pressure, few settings can rival that of a Senate confirmation hearing. Partisan battle lines are drawn, tactics are formulated, and in some instances, the drama plays out nationally. For those on the Senate Judiciary Committee, hearings provide a rare prime-time stage and an opportunity to capture that one moment that makes a political splash nationally. Or, to make a huge bellyflop.

The latter happened to New Jersey Senator Cory Booker on several occasions. "Senator Spartacus," as he came to be known, often wears his emotions on his sleeve, or so he'd have people believe.

Take, for starters, Booker's emotional deluge unleashed upon then-Homeland Security Secretary Kirstjen Nielsen for her failure to care about minority Americans (Desanctis, 2018) after an allegation that President Donald Trump used vulgarities when referring to African countries:

> *When Dick Durbin called me I had tears of rage when I heard about his experience in this meeting, and for you not to feel that hurt and that pain and to dismiss some of the questions of my colleagues ... when tens of millions of Americas are hurting right now because of what they're worried about what happened in the White House, that's unacceptable to me!*
>
> *For you not to feel that hurt and that pain and to dismiss some of the questions of my colleagues saying, 'I've already answered that line of questions' when tens of millions of Americans are hurting right now because of what they're worried about right now in the White House—that's unacceptable to me.*
>
> *Your silence and your amnesia is complicity.*

(Hains, 2018). He continued his soliloquy:

> *Why is this so important? Why is this so disturbing for me? Why am I frankly seething with anger? We have this incredible nation where we have been taught that it does not matter where you're from, it doesn't matter your color, your race, your religion, it's about the content of your character.*

(Hains, 2018). You can just hear the symphony rising to crescendo as Booker achieves his rhetorical climax, can't you? Booker's anger was palpable.

It was also widely mocked. (Twitchy, 2018).

After Booker's emotional eruption receded, many ascribed his well-known presidential aspirations as the true motive behind his performance, going as far as accusing him of over-acting—a theme repeatedly revisited throughout Booker's political career.[4] Between 2001 and 2007, Booker, then a Newark city councilman on the stump to become mayor, spun tales of his experiences with a Newark drug lord named T-Bone in speeches and in news interviews (Peyser, 2000). "T-Bone" turned out to be a fictional "archetype" thug that Booker had created. (Raab, 2008).

But perhaps Booker's grandest attempt to use his emotions to inflame others happened during the confirmation hearings of Justice Brett Kavanaugh. In a show of defiance, Booker declared that he would "knowingly violate the rules" (Axelrod, 2018) of the Senate and release "committee-confidential" documents related to Kavanaugh's stance on racial profiling:

> *I am right now, before your process is finished, I am going to release the email about racial profiling, and I understand the penalty comes with potential ousting from the Senate.*
>
> *This is about the closest I'll ever have to an 'I am Spartacus' moment.*

---

4   As you'll see, Cory Booker (and indeed every Buffoon highlighted) is what we would refer to as a Hybrid Buffoon, as he exhibits several characteristics of different classifications of Buffoonery. In this case, Booker shares traits not only with The Hot Mess, but also with *Buffoonicus ambitious*, which I'll discuss later.

(Ibid.) The reference, of course, is to the story of an ancient gladiator that led a rebellion who, after his capture, was protected by his followers when they stood up and proclaimed that they were Spartacus. The only similarity that Spartacus and Booker share is that, like Spartacus faced his demise, the opposition slaughtered Booker's remaining credibility.

As it turned out, Booker's emotionally charged act of defiance was nothing of the sort. The Senate Judiciary Committee had waived any restriction (Carney, 2018) on the documents hours before Booker's daring declaration, so he neither violated any rules nor would he suffer any punishment. Oh, and the documents Booker claimed would expose Kavanaugh did quite the opposite. One email even revealed that Kavanaugh favored "effective security measures that are race-neutral." (von Spakovsky, 2018) That's a far cry from being a bigot. In the end, Booker "was desperate to wrest the day away.... Gambling everything, he won a punchline" (Parker, 2018).

Alas, dear Spartacus. It was all for naught.

I miss the old Rev. Al. The tracksuit-wearing, gold-medallion-adorned, big-hair, big-bellied Rev. Al. The Rev. Al who rose to prominence amid the racial strife in New York City.

If you're too young to know what I'm talking about, go online and watch some old clips.

Sharpton's bombastic presentation was far from the polished personality he attempts to portray today on national broadcasts. He was crass. He was rude. He was made for the "trash TV" era of the late 1980s and early 1990s, which bubbled with racially tinged undertones. Back then, Rev. Al made regular appearance on *The Morton Downey, Jr. Show*, a show known for its "vivid and loud and cartoonish weirdness" (Kogan, 2015).

Sharpton fit like a glove.

Perhaps his most famous scene of that time played out in August of 1988 during an episode taped at the Apollo Theater in Harlem where Mort sought to tackle the general theme of race relations in the United States (Washington Post, 1988). In one corner, our far-from-humble Brooklyn preacher. In the other, conservative activist, and sharp critic of Sharpton's advocacy of Tawana Brawley (Ibid.), whom I'll discuss later: Roy Innis. Sharpton wasted no time going off on Innis:

> *Mr. Innis went from a man who would challenge (authority) to a man who would curtail and kowtow and back down.*
>
> *If (authority) can make you get on your knees... fine! That's your problem. You should shut up and let those of us that have enough guts to stand up and fight, stand up and fight. Because there are some of us who investigations and indictments and arrests don't mean*

> *anything to. How you can go from a critic… to an apologist makes you suspect at best, and a sell-out in fact.*

(Ibid.) As soon as Innis started his response, Sharpton interrupted him, calling the few words Innis managed to get out "a load of crap." (Ibid.)

It was at that moment that the $#!t hit the fan. Innis was not about to be punked on TV, so he got all up in Sharpton's face. Sharpton wasn't going to be upstaged by a "sell-out," so he tried to get up out of his seat. As soon as he got up, Innis shoved Sharpton back down into his seat, sending Sharpton ass over teakettle. The incident became national news.

Having yet to find his filter, Rev. Al. freely admitted to using his own fiery emotions to manipulate people:

> *I think that hate is an emotion. I would love to use love, but if I've gotta use hate, I'll deal what my hand calls for.*

(Datoc, 2016). Nineteen-eighties Sharpton relished in being a Hot Mess, and an angry public ate it up. Every time Rev. Al's pudgy face was plastered on your TV screen, it was must-see sleaze.

CHAPTER 3

CHASING THE DRAGON: BUFFOONICUS CONTORTIUS

We've all heard the phrase that "the ends justify the means" in moments when the means to the end at issue are unsavory or stand in direct opposition to one's reason, values, or good sense. Those who choose those distasteful means may attempt to justify their choice through a series of torturous contortions of fact and opinion, commonly referred to in politics as a "flip-flop." These out-of-character choices and subsequent justifications are indications that you have encountered *Buffoonicus contortius,* commonly referred to as...

THE AGENDA GYMNAST
The dominant characteristic of the Agenda Gymnast is a desire to reach a target or goal regardless of how loathsome or personally compromising the means required to reach that target or goal may be. Agenda Gymnasts possess a particular

talent for tailoring, twisting, and bending their stated beliefs, positions, or arguments in strange and unnatural ways to rationalize the desired outcome *du jour*.

Agenda Gymnasts typically see little to no value in the means and methods necessary to reach their intended goal. Therefore, trivialities like core values, integrity, honor, and character are measured only by the mileage each offers toward reaching the desired outcome. Agenda Gymnasts mistake their personal malleability for pragmatism because, as Buffoons of all stripes want to do, they overestimate their own ability and skill, and underestimate their audience's tolerance for bull.

When not actively working toward a desired goal, the Agenda Gymnast will exhibit a deep belief in a preferred side or agenda which she/he considers to be always right and superior. You can tell when you are dealing with an Agenda Gymnast because his/her chosen political party's position is always right, even when most consider it wrong, and the opposition's opinion is always wrong, even when most consider it right.

Think of the ardent sports fan who "roots for the laundry" (Warren, 2013). How many times have you heard a baseball fan decry sports teams "buying" championships, but then cheers unabashedly when their team lands the most expensive free agents? Or the football fan who complains if a linebacker breathes too hard on "his" quarterback but will celebrate a late hit on the opposing team's passer as just "part of the game"? If you're a sports movie buff, you may recall Bob Uecker's portrayal of announcer Harry Doyle in the *Major League* movie franchise. Uecker has a comedic line in *Major League II* (Cambern, 1994) about the Cleveland Indians' off-season signing of a free agent who had just hit a home run for his new team:

You know I used to hate Parkman when he was with the A's. It's amazing how a new uniform can change your attitude about a guy.

This statement captures the *modus operandi* of the Agenda Gymnast. Like Harry Doyle, or the sports fans turning a blind eye to their team's behavior, Agenda Gymnasts largely root for the partisan laundry regardless of the player wearing it. In doing so, their identification with the team allows Agenda Gymnasts to overlook significant failings and shortcomings that would be loudly derided if observed in the opposition.

Moreover, when the Agenda Gymnast is confronted with their own deviation from past statements or actions, they typically respond in one of two ways. In some instances, an Agenda Gymnast may accuse the confronting party of making a false equivalence, claiming the present situation is somehow different than the one s/he would normally be against. On other occasions, an Agenda Gymnast might assume the air of a pragmatist, even though they would not grant an adversary the same concession. The Agenda Gymnast's rate of success in convincing people their actions are acceptable decreases as the number and magnitude of their deviations from prior behavior increases.

The road to becoming a full-blown Agenda Gymnast is much like the road taken by an addict. Their drug of choice is "winning." The cost of "winning" is paid in the currency of their credibility. When that first "hit" of winning only requires a minor loss of credibility, the decision to do it again gets easier, even when the loss of credibility increases with each false justification made. *How* the Agenda Gymnast wins becomes less and less important. The choice to hold fast to their core values becomes harder and harder the further down the path of personal destruction the Agenda Gymnasts travels. As expected, the loss of personal credibility leads to a proportional increase in BUN, as successive acts of contortion inevitably grow in BAM.

At some point, the Agenda Gymnast reaches a tipping point where either they will recognize that "chasing the dragon" has clouded their internal moral compass and start rebuilding their character, or they will become so consumed by "winning" that their personal credibility has hit zero. When the latter occurs, the Agenda Gymnast shows what she/he truly is: a Buffoon bereft of any personal moral code.

THE POLITICAL CONTORTIONS OF THE TWO BRYANS
The year is 1904, and the Democratic National Convention sees their party split down the middle. At the heart of the divide was the debate over whether the party should continue supporting the "Free Silver" plank of the party's platform, or to support the "Gold Standard" formally enacted in 1900 for which many credited the nation's latest economic recovery. In both 1896 and 1900, "Free Silver" was the glue that kept a coalition of Democrats and progressive Populists together under the banner of their past two-time presidential nominee, William Jennings Bryan.

Bryan might best be described in terms of today's politics as a cross between Bernie Sanders and Alexandria Ocasio-Cortez, but with more moderate views and an actual track record of success. Bryan was the champion of those who believed themselves the victim of income inequality. He used the social media tool of his day, the newspaper, to lead a populist movement against corporate elitism and greed, culminating in his famous "Cross of Gold" speech in 1896 (Dickinson, 1896) that united Democrats and Populists under a big tent.

But eight years later, Bryan found his populist movement in decline thanks in part to an infusion of Klondike gold that spurred a near-decade long economic recovery.

Going into the convention, the Democratic Party's power and influence had consolidated behind a more conservative wing led by New York's Tammany Hall. They considered the "money question" sufficiently settled (St. Paul Globe, 1904). But to maintain party unity, Tammany Hall still had to reckon with Bryan. With the dual tasks of securing their own nominee while rallying support from Bryan's base, Tammany Hall put forth a party platform on June 23, 1904 (Union City Courier, 1904) that, conveniently, remained silent on the "money question." As the Democratic Party adopted a blank platform, Tammany Hall also nominated a blank candidate in a New York judge named Alton B. Parker, whose long tenure on the bench had prevented him from taking any controversial political positions.

The day after his nomination, Parker sent a telegram to the convention while controversially filled in a pretty important blank:

> I regard the gold standard as firmly and irrevocably established and I shall act accordingly if the action of the convention to-day is ratified by the people. Inasmuch as the platform is silent on the subject, I deem it necessary to make this communication to the convention for its consideration, as I should feel it my duty to decline the nomination except with that understanding.

(McKee, 1904). Tammany Hall's power play was complete, and Bryan was royally screwed. Media dubbed the gambit a "sensation which had few equals in American politics." (St. Paul Globe, 1904).[5]

This scenario may resonate with some "Bernie Bros" out there who supported Sen. Bernie Sanders for president in 2016.

Remarks attributed to Bryan immediately after the convention reveal a principled hero defeated:

> [T]he triumph of the Wall street element of the party denies to the country any hope of relief on economic

---

5   This case study exposes Agenda Gymnasts on both sides of the Democratic divide. While Bryan is the main focus, let's remember that Tammany Hall was chasing what it was always chasing—the dragon of national power. As Tammany Hall is widely derided in the annals of history for using whatever means necessary (whether legal or illegal) to gain that power, it should be no surprise that this wing of the party went to such underhanded lengths to take control of the party's direction and power. Eventually, its fate was the same as Bryan's: diminished credibility.

questions. I have nothing to take back, I have nothing to withdraw of the things that I have said against the methods pursued to advance his candidacy. It was a plain and deliberate attempt to deceive the party.

The New York platform was vague and meaningless, and purposely so, because the advocates of Judge Parker were trying to secure votes from among the people who would have opposed his views had they known them. If he had sent to the Albany convention the telegram that he sent to the St. Louis convention…. He would have had…. No possible chance for the nomination. Be he and his managers adroitly and purposely concealed his position until the delegates had been corralled and the nomination assured.

(Union City Courier, 1904). Sour grapes, to be sure. But to appreciate how screwed Bryan was, you must realize how invested he was in this "Free Silver" movement. Bryan was the face of "Free Silver" much like Sanders was the face of the far-left socialist-progressive movement in 2016 and 2020. Bryan had previously written in his book *The First Battle*, in 1896 that "the gold standard is a conspiracy against the human race" and that he would "no more join the ranks of those who propose to fasten it upon the American people than I would enlist in an army which was marching to attack my home and destroy my family."

With such strong and deeply held principles, surely Bryan wouldn't go back on those words, right?

Wrong.

You see, I might have left off some additional remarks from Bryan's post-convention statement. My bad. While condemning the proceedings out of one side of his mouth, Bryan voiced support for Judge Parker in the same statement from the other side of his mouth:

> *Judge Parker stands for enough things that are good to justify me in giving him my vote…*
>
> *The nomination was secured… by crooked and indefensible methods, but the democrat who loves his country has to make his decisions upon conditions as he finds them, not upon conditions as he would like to have them."*

(Union City Courier, 1904). You feelin' me, Bernie Bros?

Bryan's supporters reacted with shock and sadness at his unthinkable betrayal:

> *Mr. Bryan tells us that he will support this gold-bug, trust-controlled ticket, but after election he will pick up the thread where he dropped it and renew his teachings along economic lines. Mr. Bryan's present position, as a champion of a gold-bug ticket, reminds us of Rip Van Winkle. Rip swore off drinking whisky, but whenever any one offered him a drink, he drank it, saying, "Well, boys, this time don't count." And then he proceeded to swear off again. With Bryan, his support of the gold-bug this time doesn't count. After election, he'll swear off again—till the next time.*

How can Mr. Bryan expect the people who believed in him so implicitly to continue to follow him?

No, Mr. Bryan. The people will never trust you so implicitly again.

(Kansas Agitator, 1904). There are even accounts of Bryan stumping for Parker in Missouri, where former supporters fully expected Bryan to "eloquently request" that the "enthusiastic silver men" who had cast over 350,000 votes for their sterling hero to transfer their allegiance to "Parker... and the goldbug telegram" (Plymouth Tribune, 1904). Headlines syndicated across newspapers in the Midwest begged the question: Were there two Bryans? (Ibid.).

Ultimately, Bryan lost standing and the 1904 election ultimately went down in history as one of the most lopsided in our nation's history, with Republican President Teddy Roosevelt trouncing Judge Parker in both the popular and electoral vote. But, while Bryan would return to prominence later in his career, his pursuit of two dragons—the Populist cause of "Free Silver" and his lofty standing in the Democratic Party—squandered personal credibility to the point that the question of whether there were "Two Bryans" lingered. (Stevenson, 1907).

THE GREAT BIPARTISAN FLIP-FLOP ON THE SUBJECT OF IMPEACHMENT

No clearer modern example exists of an Agenda Gymnast's flip-flop than the shifting views on presidential impeachment.

We start with Jerrold Nadler, a longtime Democratic congressman from "The Peoples' Republic of" New York. Nadler has the distinction of serving in Congress when it approved articles of impeachment for two different Presidents: Democrat Bill Clinton in 1998 and Republican Donald Trump in 2019.

For those who do not know, President Clinton was impeached in late 1998 for willfully corrupting and manipulating the judicial process for his personal gain and exoneration, impeding the administration of justice by providing perjurious, false, and misleading testimony to a federal grand jury concerning a number of topics (US Congress, 1998), including his relationship with a subordinate government employee named Monica Lewinsky. Maybe you've heard of her.

In any event, Nadler notably spoke against impeaching the popular President Clinton as an abuse of congressional powers for a partisan purpose intended to overturn the will of the voters:

> *The effect of impeachment is to overturn the popular will of the voters as expressed in a national election. We must not overturn an election and remove a president from office except to defend our very system of government or our constitutional liberties against a dire threat. And we must not do so without an overwhelming consensus of the American people and of their representatives in Congress of the absolute necessity.*
>
> *There must never be a narrowly voted impeachment or an impeachment substantially supported by one of our major political parties and largely opposed by the other. Such an impeachment would lack legitimacy, would produce divisiveness and bitterness in our politics for years to come. And will call into question the very legitimacy of our political institutions.*
>
> *The American people have heard all the allegations against the president, and they overwhelmingly oppose impeaching him. The people elected the president, they still support him. We have no right to overturn the considered judgment of the American people. There are clearly some members of the Republican majority who have never accepted the results of the 1992 or 1996 elections and who apparently have chosen to ignore the message of last month's election. But in a democracy, it*

> is the people who rule, not political elites, and certainly not those members of political elites who will not be here in the next election and the next Congress having been repudiated at the polls. Some members of this committee may think the people have chosen badly; but it is the people's choice and we must respect it absent the fundamental threat to our democratic form of government that would justify overturning the repeated expression of the people's will at the ballot box.

(Wall Street Journal, 2019). If I didn't let you know Nadler said this, you'd be forgiven for crediting statements to a Trump supporter during the first impeachment of President Trump in 2020. You'd also be forgiven for crediting the next statement to today's Democratic leadership. But it is not:

> You don't... have to be convicted of a crime to lose your job in this constitutional republic if this body determines that your conduct as a public official is clearly out of bounds in your role.
>
> Because impeachment is not about punishment. Impeachment is about cleansing the office. Impeachment is about restoring honor and integrity to the office.

(CNN, 1999). Former congressman and current senator Lindsey Graham uttered these words. He served as one of the House managers in the Clinton impeachment. Graham was also an ardent Trump supporter and confidant.

Oh, how the tables turned a generation later.

Republicans and Democrats found themselves arguing against their positions from a generation ago during the first Trump impeachment. Both Nadler and Graham seemingly had a change of mind and adopted the other's position. Now, Nadler is concerned "the integrity of the United States democratic process" (US Congress, 1998), and it is Graham decrying a partisan witch hunt:

> The desire to impeach President Trump began the day he was sworn in as president. The fix was in.
>
> This will be the first impeachment in American history driven by partisan politics and not an outside investigation. I fear House Democrats are turning impeachment into a tool to be used when you don't like a president's policies or style.

(Graham, 2019). I guess everyone in Washington owns a pair of flip-flops.

It is not a stretch to claim that Rev. Al Sharpton has not been the most ardent supporter of law enforcement. In fact, a video from 1992 shows Sharpton giving a somewhat tongue-in-cheek speech that one could easily construe as encouraging violence against the police. (Dowling, 2016). While Sharpton did not outright call on supporters to go out and kill cops, he used derogatory phrases against the police that should not be used in civil company. Sharpton also insinuated that big-talkers who actually threatened violence against the police didn't have the fortitude to make good on their threats. "You ain't offed one of them. What I believe in I do," Sharpton is heard saying (Ibid.).

So it came as a surprise to many when news broke that Rev. Al was an informant for the FBI.

According to published reports, Rev. Al worked with the FBI in the 1980s as part of an investigation targeting boxing promoter Don King. (Hartmann, 2014). As the story goes, Sharpton was pressed into service after he had gotten himself caught up in a drug sting (Campanile, 2014).

Faced with an image dilemma (the importance of which we'll discuss in the next chapter) for turning snitch, Rev. Al did what he does best: contort the facts. "I was not and am not a rat because I wasn't with the rats, I'm a cat. I chase rats," declared Rev. Al, attempting to separate himself from the criminal underworld in which he had been ensnared (Antenucci, 2014). Once again, Sharpton became the hero of his own story:

> You had two options: Get killed by the mob…or get killed or hurt for trying to get them out of the community. Or the other option was to leave things how they were, and I was not about to do that….

(Campanile, 2014). And, of course, Sharpton played the role that has defined his life—a victim of discrimination:

> *The idea that blacks can't speak out because they'd be labeled snitches amounts to stereotyping and criminalizing.... It's another way of using the n-word on us, that we're just savages.... If I talked about a corrupt assemblyman in East Harlem, that is good government. But if I'm talking about mobsters, I'm Reverend Rat? Give me a break.*

(Antenucci, 2014).

Truly a master's class in agenda gymnastics.

CHAPTER 4

LOST IN ALL THEIR GLORY: BUFFOONICUS OBLIVIOUS

This next Buffoon may be the most relatable. Not to get all psychological on you, but I am willing to bet that we have all experienced, to varying degrees, moments that deflated our egos and took us down a peg in our own estimation. It can be something as small as the embarrassment of looking for your glasses when they were on top of your head the whole time (which I cannot tell you how many times a day that happens to me!), or something as significant as—and I am just spit-balling here—a white female presidential candidate on a hip-hop radio talk show boasting how she carries a bottle of hot sauce in her purse at all times (Itay, 2016).

I immediately think of my own experiences with a certain former congressman-turned-convict named Michael Grimm (R-NY). His perfect pinstriped suits and matinee idol looks created a bulletproof veneer, which screamed electability. What a shame… all that work to mask the arrogant person he was. Alas, the "beauty" was only skin deep, as all his personal faults were ultimately exposed.

Such is the nature of this Buffoon, who makes foolish decisions based either on hyper-awareness of one's self image or a total lack of self-awareness. This is the core of…

THE POLITICAL NARCISSIST

While the name probably gives it away, it really is uncanny how the evident characteristics of the Political Narcissist's mirrors some of the clinical symptoms of the personality disorder. But take caution: As I've mentioned in other chapters, I am neither a doctor nor a therapist, and I will not pretend to diagnose any individual Buffoon we discuss with any physical, mental, or psychological condition. That said, let's keep the clinical definition in mind:

> *Narcissistic personality disorder—one of several types of personality disorders—is a mental condition in which people have an inflated sense of their own importance, a deep need for excessive attention and admiration, troubled relationships, and a lack of empathy for others. But behind this mask of extreme confidence lies a fragile self-esteem that's vulnerable to the slightest criticism.*
>
> *People with narcissistic personality disorder may be generally unhappy and disappointed when they're not given the special favors or admiration [which] they believe they deserve. They may find their relationships unfulfilling, and others may not enjoy being around them.*

(Mayo Clinic, 2022). Sound familiar?

Every politician is trained to protect their public image at all costs because politicians and their handlers believe their outward image is vital to their career advancement. One becomes a Political Narcissist when the politician starts to "believe their own hype," or when maintaining their personal narrative becomes more important than fulfilling the responsibilities of their given political position. Thus, a Political Narcissist reveals him/herself through manifesting behavior motivated primarily by being in and/or remaining in political power.

At this tipping point, the Political Narcissist's attitude shifts from public service to political perception. She/he develops an air of superiority and/or irreproachability, which she/he neither earned nor deserved based on merit. Of course, this new "superiority complex" projects a false image, as reasonable people know that no politician is neither superior nor irreproachable because they, like us, are fallible and, more importantly, answerable to the people they serve. Signs that you are dealing with a Political Narcissist include dismissiveness, frequent impatience, and increased agitation, but confirmation only occurs when his/her false portrayal is exposed, yet the subject stubbornly presses on his/her desired path, nonetheless. As the saying goes in Proverbs 16:18, "[p]ride goeth before destruction, and a haughty spirit before a fall."

Do not confuse random acts of political narcissism with positively identifying a Political Narcissist. The Political Narcissist's false self-image is ingrained in their psyche to the point of near-total dependency on it. A subject must display a prolonged dedication to the observed falsity, a total lack of interest in personal change or growth (which can lead to the subject developing secondary characteristics of *Buffoonicus contortius*, also known as the Agenda Gymnast), and a dismissive attitude toward outside challenges to their falsity before we can conclude that one is a Political Narcissist.

Senator Ted Cruz (R-TX) is a prime example. He most definitely committed an act of political narcissism when he abandoned his native Texas during a freak cold snap and snowstorm to take his family to Cancun for the weekend (Parker, 2021).

As the story goes, after much of Texas lost power and heat, Cruz and his wife organized a trip to warmer climates to escape the perils his constituents were facing. Cruz compounded matters when he attempted to "save face" by claiming his daughters had asked to go on a trip with friends and he just "wanted to be a good dad" (Mazza, 2021), and had only planned to escort his family to their destination safely and return. Yet airline records showed that Cruz had changed his return ticket date only after the controversy arose. Cruz immediately apologized for his actions (Peoples, et. al., 2021), admitted that he intended to "work remotely" through the weekend, and eventually, the embarrassment subsided (Desiderio, et al, 2021).

Clearly, this shattered Cruz's self-made image of being a tireless public servant for his state and country because a person with those virtues would not go on a vacation in a middle of a crisis. However, Cruz was effectively contrite after the whole situation came to light:

> I have to admit, I started having second thoughts almost the moment I sat down on the plane. Frankly, leaving when so many Texans were hurting didn't feel right, and so I changed my return flight and flew back on the first available flight I could take.

(Ibid.). Cruz's near-immediate snap back to the reality of his Buffoonish acts saved him from being classified as a full-fledged Political Narcissist and saved him from the Sharpton-esque range for this particular act's BAM—for now. But our pseudoscience demands close observation for signs of future BUN growth.

THE "APOLLO OF THE SENATE" BECOMES THE BUTT OF HIS OWN JOKE

It is March of 1884. In a courthouse in Manhattan, one of the largest—if not *the* largest—probate disputes to date in American history is playing out before an audience both in the gallery and in print media. Mary Irene Hoyt, daughter of multimillionaire Jesse Hoyt, was contesting her late father's multimillion dollar will.

Don't worry, I won't burden you with the complexities of late-nineteenth century probate law. The players in this little drama are far more important. Former US Secretary of State William M. Evarts represented the proponents of Hoyt's will, and former US senator, Roscoe Conkling appeared on behalf of Ms. Hoyt. Why were such heavy hitters of their time facing off over a rather routine testamentary dispute? It might have had something to do with the valuation of the estate hanging in the balance reaching today's equivalent of hundreds of millions of dollars.

But for the rest of the people with nothing at stake in this matter, this family drama of the rich and famous was the reality show entertainment of its time, playing out in public for all to see.

The focus of our attention is Mr. Conkling. Now in private practice, the "Apollo of the Senate" (US Senate, 2021) was, by many accounts, a brilliant statesman, a capable orator, and a political power broker *par excellence* (Depew, 1922) who many credit for the election of President Chester A. Arthur. (US Senate, 2021). Conkling was also the prototypical Political Narcissist: "[A] vain and haughty man with a monumental ego, [Conkling] believed himself unfettered by the rules that governed lesser mortals" (Wolff, 1997). Indeed, Chauncey M. Depew, wrote in his 1922 memoir:

> *Roscoe Conkling was created by nature for a great career. That he missed it was entirely his own fault.*

> *[H]is intolerable egotism deprived him of vision necessary for supreme leadership. With all his oratorical power and his talent for debate, he made little impression upon the country and none upon posterity.*

Returning to the courtroom, the *New York Times* memorialized a portion of Conkling's cross-examination of the writer of the Hoyt will, attorney Cornelius Van Santvoord:

> "Was not Jesse Hoyt in later years one of the largest and boldest grain operators in the East?" asked Mr. Conkling.
>
> "He was one of the largest," Mr. Van Santvoord replied, "but I can't say one of the boldest. He was generally successful, but he made some mistakes."
>
> "Oh, well," said Mr. Conkling pleasantly, "all great men make mistakes sometimes."
>
> There was a roar of laughter in response, and the ex-Senator seemed to realize that the laugh was on himself.

(New York Times, 1884).

Why would Conkling realize that the crowd's roar of laughter was *at* him and not *with* him? As with all comedy, context is key. Understanding the context takes us back to the summer of 1879 in Narragansett, Rhode Island.

"Oh, well. All great men make mistakes sometimes."
Roscoe Conkling (R-NY) portrayed as a Buffoon
on the cover of Puck Magazine.
(US Senate, 1884).

It is here where we meet Kate Chase. The daughter of Salmon P. Chase, Lincoln's Secretary of Treasury, Washington society-types considered Chase to be the most respected and prominent lady (New England Historical Society, 2022). She was the Kardashian of her time: beautiful and ambitious (Kearns-Goodwin, 2006). She married well in 1863 to former Rhode Island Governor and US Senator William Sprague (New England Historical Society, 2022).

Ah, Kate and William. A pairing of nineteenth-century American royalty. Just to give you the sense of the pomp surrounding this union, the band at their wedding played "The Kate Chase March" during the processional, a number written just for Kate (Moser, 2019). Yes, it was that big of a deal.

To cut completely to the... ahem... Chase, over the years, our dear Mr. Conkling would pay visits to the very-married young woman at Canonchet, the Sprague's summer home in Narragansett. As the story goes, it was August 8, 1879:

> *Mr. Conkling was once forbidden by Mr. Sprague to come to Canonchet. Despite this, however, the Executive [Sprague] later met the Senator [Conkling] on the estate coming from the rear of the house—some reports had it that the Senator jumped from a window—and after him came the Governor with his old civil war musket in his hands.*

(New York Times, 1909). Sprague had caught Conkling, the senatorial Apollo, and his wife *in flagrante delicto* in Sprague's bedroom! (Bell, 2014). It was the scandal of the decade.

Conkling went into full damage control mode to save his image. He even put up a patsy named George Linck to publicly claim to be the victim of Sprague's misunderstanding (New England Historical Society, 2022). Conflicting reports sprang up from different newspapers across the Northeast, which the stories eventually coming back around to Conkling, especially after Linck recanted his story (Ibid.). The *New York Graphic* soon declared:

> *The story of the Naragansett Pier scandal, as all details are made public, places Senator Roscoe Conkling in*

an extremely awkward position. *Unless he can clear himself, he will stand convicted of having stolen another man's house with the intention of destroying the peace and happiness of that home. His conduct when confronted by the bereaved husband bears the stamp of cowardice. Lechery and cowardice cannot be forgiven in a person assuming to occupy a high public position. We very much believe that in Rhode Island lies the grave of Roscoe Conkling's political future.*

(Ibid.; The Weekly Union Times, 1879). I think my favorite coverage of the incident comes from the *Iowa Press*, which should be read along with the tune of the famous nursery rhyme playing in your head:

> *Sing a song of Shot Gun*
> *Belly full of rye*
> *Two loyal Senators making mud pie*
> *When the pie was opened*
> *The public got a smell*
> *And Sprague said to Conkling*
> *Now you go to H-ll*

Moser, 2019). By the following year, Conkling's national political aspirations had fizzled, and Kate and William were divorced (Ibid.).

So, now you have the source and context of the uproarious laughter that Conkling suffered in that Manhattan courtroom some years later Conkling may have forgotten himself, but the public had not. What a shining example of a shocking lack of self-awareness.

With the benefit of living one hundred years of hindsight, I dare say that Mr. Depew may have been incorrect. While many of the achievements of Roscoe Conkling, the statesman, are reserved to the memories of the political wonks like yours truly, posterity did retain some memory of Mr. Conkling, the Political Narcissist.

FAUXCAHONTAS'S "BIG" REVEAL

Family heritage is important to many people. Rituals and traditions passed down through the generations give us a connection to our past and an identity that can become a source of personal pride. This can be said to be true of Senator Elizabeth Warren (D-MA).

As far back as 1986, Warren self-identified as Native American. The earliest known proof of Warren's claimed ancestry was a registration card she filled out and filed with the State Bar of

Texas (Linksey, 2019). Warren later claimed "minority" status within the Association of American Law Schools' directory from when it first highlighted minority professors in 1986 until 1995 (Ibid.). While working for the University of Pennsylvania, she made it a point to change her ethnic identity from white to Native American (Ibid.). She did the same while working at Harvard Law School. From 1995 through 2004, Harvard listed Warren as Native American in its federal affirmative action forms (Ibid.) and lauded her as Harvard Law's "first woman of color" on the faculty (Padilla, 1997).

Clearly, Warren's claimed ethnicity became ingrained in her own self-image and personal identity, and acted as a virtue signal for herself and the academic aristocracy who could tout Warren's "diversity."

This is all well and good, except Warren is, outwardly, a blue-eyed, blonde-haired, well-to-do, privileged white woman.

Political adversaries first called Warren's claimed heritage into question during her 2012 run for US Senate. Warren held fast to her self-image (Poor, 2012) of Cherokee and Delaware Indian ancestry, (Francke-Buta, 2012) stating, "[t]hese are my family stories. This is what my brothers and I were told by my mom and my dad, my mammaw and my pappaw. This is our lives. And I'm very proud of it" (Nickisch, 2012).

Unfortunately, stories from "mammaw" and "pappaw" don't cut it. Questions lingered for years, especially after Warren couldn't name any specific Native American ancestor and a report of proof vindicating Warren turned out to be a bust (Francke-Buta, 2012).

Years later, with Warren seen as a strong 2020 presidential contender after winning re-election to the Senate in 2018, President Donald Trump returned to the question of Warren's claimed heritage with the abrasive zeal and gusto for which has been a hallmark of his own political career. Adopting the nickname "Pocahontas" for Warren, Trump boastfully claimed he would pay (insert your best Dr. Evil's voice here) one million dollars to the charity of Warren's choice if she could produce DNA evidence proving mammaw and pappaw right (Asma, 2018).

Amazingly, Warren's political narcissism compelled her to take the bait.

In an elaborate series of documentary-styled videos featuring interviews of family, friends, students, former colleagues (Zhang, 2018), Warren did a grand unveil of a DNA analysis conducted by Stanford University, which concluded that while "the great majority of (Warren's) identifiable ancestry is European" (Dewberry, 2018), there was evidence that "strongly support[s] the existence of an unadmixed Native American ancestor in the individual's pedigree, likely in the range of six to ten generations ago" (Asma, 2018).

Boom goes the dynamite, right? Unfortunately for Warren, the dynamite blew right in her face.

Six to ten generations? That would make Warren no more than 1/67 Native American at best, and 1/1024 at worst. (Linskey, 2018). More importantly, the Cherokee Nation viewed Warren's videos as nothing but kabuki theater, calling Warren's DNA presentation "useless."

> Using a DNA test to lay claim to any connection to the Cherokee Nation or any tribal nation, even vaguely, is inappropriate and wrong. It makes a mockery out of DNA tests and its legitimate uses while also dishonoring legitimate tribal governments and their citizens, whose ancestors are well documented and whose heritage is proven. Senator Warren is undermining tribal interests with her continued claims of tribal heritage.

(Dewberry, 2018). Warren would issue an apology to the Cherokee Nation (Steinbuch, 2019), but not for the reasons she should have. Because Warren's assumed heritage was immovable within her political self-image, she confused genetics for culture. Essentially, Warren appropriated Native American culture and iconography and dragged it through the mud as a means to preserve her political self-image (Moya-Smith, 2019). In doing so, Warren created a dog-and-pony spectacle that should have never happened.

The political calculus was all bad. Democrat allies openly wondered what would possess Warren to so something as stupid as releasing such a dud of a reveal just weeks before the 2018 midterm elections, fearing the potential collateral damage (Concha, 2018).

Not even anti-Trump media outlet *CNN* could spin Warren's unveiling positively:

> In the after-action report, it was clear how badly Warren's strategy had failed: Rather than get the issue off the table in advance of the start of the 2020 campaign,

she had pushed her heritage (and the questions around it) into the national spotlight, offered nothing even close to definitive proof of anything and, in so doing, made herself an incredibly ripe target for the President of the United States.

(Cilliza, 2018).

Ultimately, Warren's unforced error borne of her political narcissism did nothing but give President Trump his victory over Fauxcahontas.

IMAGE ABOVE ALL

I do not presume to know Rev. Al. I doubt that more than a handful actually *know* Rev. Al. I mean, *really* know him.

Rev. Al is an ever-evolving image machine. In one decade, he's a shuckin'-and-jivin', foul-mouthed street preacher. In another, he is a candidate for office demanding to be taken seriously. In yet another, he plays the part of a polished television personality that lacks any polish at all. Is any other political personality more conscious or protective over his political self-image?

But what do we find when peering under the image?

Consider these up-close and personal observations of a former Sharpton confidante, Dr. Lenora Fulani, which she shared online in 2003:

> *During my nearly 20-year history with him… I have seen him set aside the visionary for the viable. I have seen him try to recreate himself as a progressive, out of expedience—not principle. I have seen him become what is, sadly, a second-rate Black leader.*
>
> *Sharpton, while rejecting the establishment in general… was also irresistibly drawn to the limelight. Carefully cultivating his public image as the voice of the Black citizenry, he was almost oblivious to whether the political base gathering around him could be empowered in new ways, rather than simply used to bolster his own political ascendancy.*

Because the image is where the money is, as Bob McManus so bluntly and accurately wrote in the *New York Post* in 2019:

> *Al Sharpton has been making a good living for 35 years now, pushing New York and the nation as far as his bullhorn audacity will carry him—which is pretty damned far for a one-time FBI informer who started with nothing and brought even less to the table.*
>
> *If they ever build a Con Man Hall of Fame, Alfred Charles Sharpton Jr. must be an inaugural inductee.*

The only constant portrayal throughout the decades have been Rev. Al, the activist. He's a man of the people, and a man for *his* people. That is why when there is a racial crisis somewhere in America, Rev. Al will be there. But, instead of traveling coach he's arriving in a private jet, which he once boastfully (or unconsciously) posted on Twitter (Twitter, 2021). That's one of many indelible images that pierce through the self-image of Rev. Al, man of the people, into Rev. Al the Conman.

PART II

THE BÊTE NOIRE

CHAPTER 5

SUCCUBI AND SNOLLYGOSTERS: BUFFOONICUS PARASITOS

So when I came across "snollygoster," I knew this absurdly fun word would be the perfect descriptive term for the parasites in politics who get involved to feed their egos and bank accounts.

The definition and origin of "snollygoster" is a little tough to nail down. In some texts, a snollygoster is defined as "a pretentious boaster," and a "fellow who wants office, regardless of party, platform or principle, and who, whenever he wins, gets there by the sheer force of *monumental talknophical assumnacy*" (Wilder, 1998).

If someone can tell me what those last two words mean, I'd greatly appreciate it.

The word seems to originate from the American south in the 1850s "to refer derogatorily and somewhat humorously to a politician" (Merriam-Webster, 2022). By the 1890s, Colonel H. W. Ham of Georgia would stump across his state giving a very entertaining speech where he refined the definition to "one with an unquenchable thirst for office with neither the power to get it nor the ability to fill it" (Hicky, 1957). Later, President Harry S. Truman would revive the word as an epithet toward "political shysters"(Ibid.). This fun word would have been lost to history if not for Bill O'Reilly (Dwyer, 2017).

It is Colonel Ham's definition that neatly fits our next classification of Buffoon. They are the perennial candidates, the gadflies, and the personification of so many other caricatures of the political grifters. They are collectively the lower political class we call…

THE LEECHES
The Leech is an unprincipled person "who is continually side-wiping around after a little office which he can't get, and which he ain't got sense enough to fill if he could get it" (Hicky, 1957). This Buffoon starts as a nobody with a low BUN score because she/he has no real bona fide credentials to hold office or any real public visibility. The Leech will then latch onto some larger political entity and, by doing so, hopes to benefit from their proximity thereto. Think of the commensalism between a whale and a barnacle, but more devious. Like the barnacle, the Leech attaches to its chosen political target, finds stability, gets a free ride, and has access to the "inside baseball" of politics. Of course, the larger the

whale, the greater the number of Leech barnacles will attempt to attach themselves. Also, the higher the political stakes, the greater the field of Leeches widens to include not only these lower hangers-on, but also unqualified political hacks and lesser politicians.

The benefit to a host to allow the Leech to gravitate and linger is minimal. A Leech may begin as a regular office volunteer, a seat-filler attending an event, or will walk the neighborhood dropping your literature with minimal care. But the price for the Leech's minimal offerings can be steep, as she/he will expect undeserved access in return, such as favors, unlimited photo ops, and ultimately, money, prestige, and power that she/he would not be able to achieve alone.

But unlike a barnacle, the Leech seeks to shark up, and when they do, will disregard their previous beneficial allegiance in search of their next host. Their need for personal gain leads to the inevitable compromise of whatever values they had. When the Leech attains some power, politics becomes more about angles and optics. Speaking engagements take precedence over community meetings. Their mentality breeds sloppiness, which, over time, may invariably result in more Buffoonish acts that carry a higher BAM, which, in turn, results in increased BUN growth. Alternatively, a Leech's growth stagnates, and s/he moves on to green pastures; still, other times, many Leeches find a secure position to fester and grow fat on the pure intentions of others.

The best cultural portrayal of Leeches is the movie *The Distinguished Gentleman*, Jonathan Lynn's wonderful comedy form 1992 starring Eddie Murphy about a conman elected to Congress thanks to name recognition he borrowed from the deceased former office holder who passed while diddling his legislative aide. When Murphy's character gets called out with his own rap sheet, he reveals Washington's big con:

> [E]verything else on this list is real. I did it, don't deny it. But all of this is NOTHING compared to all the $#!t I pulled off right here in Washington. And everything I did in this town would be considered legit!

(Leirer, et. al., 1992). This is "the game" that Leeches love to play: Politics is the means to their personal end.

THE "BAD BOY MAYOR OF NEWBURYPORT"
> *In the late '20s, a Buffoon of a mayor named "Bossy" Gillis put Newburyport on many a front page with his antics.*

(Time, 1947). The city of Newburyport, Massachussetts, takes pride in being the birthplace of the US Coast Guard (City of Newburyport, 2021). Whether they also take pride in being the home of its six-term mayor Andrew Joseph ("Bossy") Gillis depends on who you ask.

Bossy Gillis was born and raised in Newburyport (New York Times, 1965). After returning home from World War I, Gillis requested a permit to open a gas station, which the city denied (Ibid.). But a little thing that bureaucracy would not stop Gillis, who protested the decision by decorating "his vacant lot with tombstones and household crockery labeled:

'The Spirit of Newburyport'" (Time, 1928). One such tombstone bore the name of then-mayor Michael Cashman (New York Times, 1965). When Cashman confronted Gillis about it, Gillis walloped him (Ibid.).

I tell you, if you've never socked a mayor in the mush, you've missed half the joy in life.

And so began the long political career of a self-centered Leech. Gillis would spend two months in jail for that shot, all while denouncing "the fossils that run this burg" (Time, 1928). Gillis first ran for mayor to get back at those fossils, and "[w]ithout knowing quite why, Newburyport elected him" (Ibid.), and would do so six times over.

Gillis wasted no time carrying out his vendetta against those "fossils" because "[w]hat the hell! We won, didn't we? Don't the winner deserve the gravy?" (Ibid.). Political office didn't mellow Gillis, who "thought nothing of a fist fight or two; in fact, he said later, he cleared up more arguments by 'squarin' off' with some of his political opponents than just by 'talking'" (Reading Eagle, 1937). While Bossy loved his newly won title, he couldn't be bothered with correspondence from people who "must think I got nothing to do but open envelopes" (Time, 1928)

But in all the fun, the newly elected Gillis still "ignored the formality of obtaining a permit" (Reading Eagle, 1937) for his gas station (New York Times, 1965) and was convicted six months after taking office. The prosecutor observed that Bossy was "a willful, empty-headed boy who has never grown up. His election was an unfortunate accident. It has gone to his head. I feel that what he needs is a hot application of the law to take down the cranial swelling." (New York Times, 1928).

Yet jail was not the end of Gillis, a.k.a. "Prisoner 48866" (Ibid.). Though he served two months in jail (one at hard labor) for operating an illegal filling station, he was still the mayor. The Newburyport city government had no provision for his impeachment or removal (Ibid.). So Bossy multitasked, running the city and doing the jail's laundry at the same time (New York Times, 1965). Upon his release, Gillis's supporters greeted him with a brass band and a torchlight parade—all on his way to winning re-election (Ibid.).

Bossy may have entered politics for "vindication" (Reading Eagle, 1937), but over time, running Newburyport became a "headache" not worth the "[p]in money" of his salary (Ibid.). Still, Bossy persisted for purely parasitic purposes:

> I gotta protect my interests. I'm one of this city's heaviest taxpayers and I can't afford to have the taxes go sky-looping from here to....

(Ibid.). Of course, Gillis supplemented his "pin money" like the politicians of today, with the odd paid speaking engagement for a few grand here and there, along with starting his newspaper and publishing an autobiography simply titled *Me*. (Ibid.).

All totaled, Bossy Gillis served six non-consecutive terms as mayor and ran unsuccessfully another fourteen times. His last unsuccessful bid ended shortly before his death in 1965.

Gillis took it all in stride, proclaiming, "If they don't want Bossy Gillis after six terms, then the hell with them" (New York Times, 1965).

Public service at its finest, right?

Gillis fits most of the earmarks of a Leech: He's a perennial gadfly of a candidate who ran for office for the sake of holding it for personal gain. But opinions vary over Bossy's legacy. To some, "Gillis was one of Newburyport's great giants" and "a man of great character—always doing a kindness and never mentioning it after it was done" (Lagoulis, 2012). Others claim to have seen right through Gillis:

> *People fall for that thing, "Oh, he's a man of the people," but people didn't gain from it. They'd have him in for two terms and throw him out and have him in again. It was ridiculous.*

(Brown, 2010). Regardless, Gillis left such an indelible cultural mark that over fifty years after his passing, people still fondly recall growing up near Newburyport whose parents would chide them facetiously, "Who do you think you are, Bossy Gillis?" whenever they got a bit uppity ("Priscilla Portillo", 2021).

THE PROGRESSIVE PARASITE FROM QUEENS

Alexandria Ocasio-Cortez doesn't leech off any one person, but an entire movement.

First, consider her narrative. Prior to running for Congress, Ocasio-Cortez's political experience was as a volunteer organizer on Bernie Sanders's 2016 presidential campaign (Ocasio-Cortez, 2021). And, of course, there's her bartending and waitressing credentials, all of which propelled AOC to an upset win over a complacent longtime incumbent in a district with changed demographics.

Next, let's focus on two positions that have been a central message to AOC's reputation as a champion of socialism. AOC advocates to "tax the rich" by raising the marginal tax rate on the richest Americans to 70 percent because the so-called "one percent" do not pay their fair share (Cox, 2019). Moreover, Ocasio-Cortez hits the socialist high notes on capitalism in general:

> *Capitalism is an ideology of capital—the most important thing is the concentration of capital and to seek and maximize profit...so to me capitalism is irredeemable.*

(Warren, 2019). Pretty standard socialist fare. What is not standard is how AOC chose methods of advocacy intended more to create outrage than to reach a policy goal.

Instead of building consensus on plans to actually "tax the rich," AOC chose more unorthodox tactics, like attending the thirty-five-thousand-dollars-per-ticket Met Gala wearing a custom designer dress emblazoned with her message on it (Kurtz, 2021). It was, literally and figuratively, not a good look for AOC to be seen posing on the red carpet alongside decadent celebrities who, to quote Jerry Seinfeld from his book in 2020, looked like "Senators from Krypton" preening in outfits that stirred serious *Hunger Games* vibes. Even worse, the designer of the dress, Aurora James, turned out to be a business owner who failed to pay her fair share of taxes (Levine, 2021).

Moreover, AOC's words on capitalism ring hollow, as she has fully immersed herself in that "irredeemable" system by operating an online store peddling overpriced wares. A fifty-eight-dollar "Tax the Rich" sweatshirt is a living oxymoron (Ritschel, 2020).

Maybe AOC's unorthodox tactics actually got results. So, I looked up her congressional record and found that AOC had none. As a member of the majority in the 116th Congress, AOC sponsored twenty-three bills (US Congress, 2021). Not one made it to a vote in committee, let alone on the House floor. As I write this sentence, no AOC-sponsored legislation has passed even in the 117th Congress (US Congress, 2022). Zero. Zilch. Nada.

With no real record to speak of, Ocasio-Cortez subsists like other political bottom feeders: By using her forked tongue and image to manipulate supporters. In 2021 alone, Ocasio-Cortez parlayed her image into six million dollars in campaign and PAC contributions (Open Secrets, 2021), not to mention the free promotion by a news media on both sides of the political divide desperate to exploit virtually every breath she takes. Her social media management is impressive, to say the least, where she defines her own brand and uses opposition viewpoints to harden her own supporter base (Benwell, 2019). Just the fact that I refer to Ocasio-Cortez as "AOC" is proof that her branding works.

It is also proof positive that AOC is a near-perfect modern-day "snollygoster."

When Rev. Al ran for the Democratic Party nomination for president in 2004, his political resume did not inspire confidence in his competency. Being a child preacher at age four, an ordained minister by age ten, a youth leader with Rev. Jesse Jackson, and a friend of James Brown did not help make a polished political record (CNN, 2004). Neither did losing primary elections in two different US Senate races and one race for New York City mayor (Berggren, 2021). Still, Rev. Al threw his hat—and his inordinately big mouth—into the ring.

Sharpton was the most negatively received candidate. Forty-nine percent of Americans held a negative view of him while only 16 percent viewed him positively (CNN, 2003). Nationally, Rev. Al topped polls at 7 percent. (Ibid.)

Rev. Al did have the art of double-talk nailed. He initially claimed, "I'm not running an African-American campaign" when interviewed in late 2003, (Ibid.) but reverted to his safe space as the self-anointed voice of Black America by March of 2004:

> *I'm not running for a job; I'm running for a cause. I'm not running for a season; I'm running for a reason. I want to make sure we are never marginalized again. I want to make sure we [African-Americans] are never marginalized again.*

(McCarthy, 2004). Of course, pursuing the "cause" required Rev. Al to wine and dine in five-star hotels even while campaign resources were deep in the red (Ibid.). Typical Rev. Al.

Rather than participating in caucuses in Iowa and New Hampshire, Rev. Al focused on getting out African American votes in South Carolina. It didn't work. Thirty-seven percent of Black voters chose South Carolina's John Edwards, while another thirty-four percent chose the eventual presidential nominee, John Kerry (Kornacki, 2019). Sharpton won a paltry 17 percent of those voters (Ibid.). That means two lily-white, uber-privileged candidates each doubled Rev. Al's total, providing statistical proof that he was far from being the voice of Black America.

Nonetheless, like the true Buffoon he is, Sharpton claimed success in South Carolina (Ibid.).

CHAPTER 6

FOR THE CULTURE: BUFFOONICUS CELEBRITAS

Though he does not claim the honor of creating it, Democratic political strategist Paul Begala has been widely credited with this pithy turn of phrase, "Washington is Hollywood for the ugly people" (Washington Post, 2010). Begala keenly observed the "needy quality that actors and politicians have" (Ibid.).

Years later, Republican firebrand Andrew Breitbart turned a phrase of his own about the synergy between politics and the entertainment world when he remarked, "Politics is downstream from culture" ("Joe Rogan Experience #1525—Tim Dillon", 2020).

Recognizing that political change flows from cultural change (Kronen, 2018), both the celebrity and the politician swim the same intoxicating stream toward the allure of greater cultural influence from opposite directions, the celebrity heading downstream seeking to stave off their dimming stature caused by age or decline and the politician endeavoring upstream to break on through the barrier into mainstream consciousness.

Understanding the rationale of the so-called "Breitbart Doctrine" is the key to understanding the motivations of our next class of Buffoon...

THE CULTURE WARRIOR
As you probably already guessed, two types of Culture Warrior exist: the entertainer turned toward politics, and the politician seeking celebrity. Because of their unique place in society's social strata, our main focus will be on the entertainer-turned-politician.

The character traits of a Culture Warrior are not much different than the average Buffoons we already discussed; they can possess any combination of traits from those Lesser Hypocrites. What makes this Buffoon unique is that even their most insignificant displays of Buffoonery carry a disproportionately higher Buffoonish Action Magnitude (BAM). That is because the Culture Warrior's fame give them greater cache, especially in today's society, which places such cultural significance on their every move. It is in this respect that measuring BAM is like measuring how big of a splash you make when jumping in a pool; Culture Warriors just make a bigger splash than others. When paired with their relative political inexperience, the Culture Warrior's desperation to remain relevant often results in highly visible missteps that carry a higher-than-average BAM, thanks to their higher-than-average public visibility.

Observance of past and present entertainers entering politics reveals that many of this variety of Culture Warrior choose to transition to political engagement as a second career to rage against the dying of their light of social influence—emphasis on the word "rage," as anger plays a key role in why entertainers chose to enter the political arena. I am sure you can think of any number of faded celebrities on social media who fit the description.

The entertainer's anger is typically stoked by a combination of frustration (perhaps from a lack of personal success) and a recent awareness of some political current event or issue (such as a *cause célèbre*, a personal belief, or even an assumed grudge) filtered through their personal partisan leanings. Regardless, this variant of Culture Warrior embarks on an emotionally charged crusade with little time devoted to verifying whether the position s/he staked out is reasonable, or even factually accurate, because doing the work to understand a given political issue is mad hard, yo. I mean, who has time for thinking? That's why they have "people" thinking for them. Specious their positions may be, the Culture Warrior proclaims their new personal truth loudly, publicly, and frequently, with no less than American society as we know it at stake.

The Culture Warrior seeks instinctive validation from his/her built-in fandom from their former exploits for every political utterance. This creates enmity with those who disagree either with their refusal to "stay in their lane" or who fundamentally disagree with the Culture Warrior's newly expressed views. Meanwhile, like-minded partisans immediately latch on to the Culture Warrior's cache and opinion as conclusive proof that their cause is right, just, and most importantly, the established cultural norm.

We should note that when the politician goes full-on Hollywood, the objective remains the same: to expand their own reach into a broader audience and to validate not only what they believe as a cultural norm, but to implant themselves into the stream of social consciousness. Appearances on late-night television, comedy skits on stage, or a guest spot on a television program are staples of the Culture Warrior's playbook—hardly bastions of civil political discourse. Spreading the Culture Warrior's ideas eventually gives way to creating a cultural presence where merely stating a political position engenders instant social approval through personality alone. Again, the laziness of the Culture Warrior wins out.

Noted celebrity-turned-podcaster Joe Rogan has made his own observations on the modern iteration of the Culture Warrior, which he suggests is just another role—to play a progressive toeing the line for the entertainment industry:

> *They find the pattern, the way they have to talk and the things they have to talk about, and they lock into those things with no deviation. They find whatever the line is where Hollywood wants. It's always Left. Always super progressive, always super woke, and they f***ing ride that line like a railroad train—no deviation, and it's so obvious.*

(Toto, August 2020). Whether left or right, entertainer or politician, the predictable pattern of Buffoonery emerges in the same fashion as the Lesser Hypocrites discussed earlier: when the pursuit of fame and adulation from an adoring public becomes the larger goal and can metastasize into a more dangerous class of Buffoon. The effect of that pursuit is often reputational damage and the reduction from mainstream social influence to bitter partisan through the same media the Culture Warrior sought to avail. Or worse, the Culture Warrior is lampooned as an archetypal caricature of their perceived role in life.

SAM WOOD'S WAR ON COMMUNISM

You wouldn't know it today, but once upon a time, Hollywood used to be filled with loud and proud conservatives as America emerged out of World War II. Names like Walt Disney, Gary Cooper, and director Victor Fleming started organizing secretly against the perceived scourge of communism. (Ceplair, 2003). Among those early organizers was a moderately successful director named Sam Wood.

In the pantheon of great Hollywood directors, Sam Wood is not the first that comes to mind. Or the second. Or even the third. Okay, let's be honest; most of you are thinking, "Sam who?" But I bet you know his work. Sam Wood is best known for directing Gary Cooper in *Pride of the Yankees*, the Marx Brothers in *A Night at the Opera* and *A Day at the Races*, and he was nominated for an Academy Award for *Goodbye, Mr. Chips* in 1939 (Barson, 2021). He even had a hand in finishing *Gone with the Wind* (Ibid.). Certainly not a career to sneeze at, but not one of acclaim, either.

Unfortunately, Wood's legacy is not his body of work alone, but includes his obsessive, almost-fanatical political crusade during the mid-twentieth century during the Red Scare. The origins of this previously apolitical figure's political awakening can be found in Wood's relationship with William Randolph Hearst, whose aggressive stances in opposition to the "dictatorial" nature of FDR's New Deal appealed to Wood (Ceplair, 2003). Wood's daughter, Jeane, witnessed firsthand how "it"—communism—twisted her father's personality:

> *He was such a charming man—gentle, generous, dear ... until 'It' came up. 'It' invariably transformed Dad into a snarling, unreasoning brute; we used to leave the dinner table with our guts tangled and churning from the experience.*

(Ibid.). Right about now, I bet you're picturing that one relative who always brings up politics at Thanksgiving.

Wood's family also believed coming short of winning the Oscar for *Mr. Chips* "galled and disappointed him beyond measure" and transformed him "from an anti-Communist to a possessed witch-hunter" (Ibid.).

With iron now in his soul (Ibid.), Wood emerged as one of many high-profile, politically conservative Hollywood film types expressing paranoia that "communists, radicals and crackpots" (Time, 1944) sought to dominate their industry (Ibid.). To combat this perceived scourge, Wood became the "generalisimo" (Ibid.) of the Motion Picture Alliance for the Preservation of American Ideals (MPA) in 1944 (Ibid.), an organization of actors, directors, writers, and producers pledging to "fight, with every means of our organized command, any effort of any group or individual, to divert the loyalty of the screen from the free America that gave it birth" (Ceplair, 2003).

Wood's tone in his first speech to the MPA may remind you of a certain former president's affinity for all things America:

> *The American motion picture industry is, and will continue to be, held by Americans for the American people, in the interests of America, and dedicated to the preservation and continuance of the American scene and the American way of life.*

(Ibid.). Six "Americas" in one sentence. Beat that, President Trump!

Wood's dislike for FDR intertwined with his Communist fixation. As his obsession grew, Wood would note the names of those Communists and supporters of FDR that must be purged from Hollywood in a "little black book" (Ibid.). Wood's fanaticism also bled into his films. *Time Magazine* said Wood "diluted *For Whom the Bell Tolls* so that Spanish Fascists became 'nationalists' and Spanish Republicans came out like the American G.O.P." (Time, 1944). Of course, he had no definitive proof that anyone was an actual subversive. Opinions were all Wood had, and those were good enough for him and those in his bubble, who pushed for Congress to root out the Communist threat in Hollywood (Watts, 2013).

Wood's lists and opinions would become the thrust of his testimony before the infamous House Un-American

Committee's opening hearing in October of 1947, which increased fears of undue Communist influence in the US film industry but amounted to nothing more than a reactionary attempt to purge political opposition. There, Wood testified of his "knowledge" that Communists were infiltrating and controlling the Screen Directors Guild (Tower, 1947) because he knows a Commie when he sees a Commie, dammit:

> *If I have any doubt that they are [Communists], then I haven't any mind. I am convinced that these Hollywood Commies are agents of a foreign country. These Communists thump their chests and call themselves liberals, but if you drop their rompers you'll find a hammer & sickle on their rear ends.*

(Time, 1947). Not exactly hard evidence. But there was such hysteria in those times, that members of Congress thanked Wood for his "guts" and "courage" in spreading his Buffoonish rumor and innuendo (Ibid.). Isn't it amazing how Buffoonery snowballs when given that first nudge down the hill of willful ignorance and opportunism?

Ultimately, Wood's obsession would be his undoing. In September of 1949, Wood got into a heated argument with actress Margaret Sullavan, who threatened to walk off his latest project if Wood had a screenwriter he accused of being a Communist removed (Dewey, 1997). With that moment stuck in his craw, Wood then received news later that evening of a slander lawsuit brought against the MPA by playwright Emmet Lavery (Ceplair, 2003). The day's frustrations were too much for Wood's heart to bear, as he collapsed and died of heart failure (Ibid.).

Amazingly, even death did not put an end to Wood's fanaticism. Wood added a clause to his will requiring heirs to file an affidavit swearing they "are not now, nor have they ever been, Communists" as a pre-condition to any inheritance (Ibid., Sbardellati, 2012).

MILANO'S TURNS FROM #METOO TO #MEBLUE

If ever an award existed for the most hysterical performance on a political stage, that award would have to go to actress-turned-activist Alyssa Milano.

Without completely revisiting the confirmation hearing for Supreme Court Justice Brett Kavanaugh, the fledging actress was front and center—literally—in the hearings chamber, seen right over the shoulder of Kavanaugh holding a "I Believe Survivors" placard as he denied allegations of sexual abuses made by Dr. Christine Blasey Ford, whom Milano supported (Strause, 2018). A self-proclaimed victim of abuse, Milano boldly claimed that allegations of assault alone, with no supporting evidence, should be enough to derail Kavanaugh's nomination:

> Every person who refuses to loudly and openly reject Brett Kavanaugh's nomination is telling every generation of Americans that an alleged abuser's career is more valuable than a survivor's humanity. And the highest court in our land is no place for an alleged sexual offender to sit.

(Andrews, 2018). Hence the familiar battle cry to "believe all women" propelled Milano into a second career in activism:

> No one in the industry shrieked louder about #MeToo, women's rights and, specifically, the Kavanaugh hearings, than the former "Charmed" star. Milano essentially rebranded herself as an actress/activist, drawing sizable media mentions with every Tweet.

(Toto, April 2020). Milano's loud political opinions certainly paid personal dividends, elevating her Twitter following to over three million (Ibid.). Apparently, those millions were not enough for Milano, who bemoaned how popular comedian and podcaster Joe Rogan carried more influence than she did (Sheffield, Jr., 2020). Rogan, a celebrity who has successfully parlayed his fame into becoming a credible cultural influencer, made reference to Milano as making ""[t]hat shift where you go from actor to activist, all in, as soon as the f***ing calls stop coming in, you're like, 'All right, I'm an activist'" ("Joe Rogan Experience #1525—Tim Dillon", 2020).

Milano's influence-measuring contest notwithstanding, many detractors took notice when Milano held her tongue while another purported victim of sexual abuse, Tara Reade, spoke her truth against then-presidential candidate and friend of Milano, Joe Biden (Rakich, 2020). To the surprise of no political observer, Reade's allegations against her former boss did not make as much of a splash in corporate media as Dr. Ford (Cherkasky, 2020).

Instead of taking a principled stance alongside Reade, Milano took up for Biden:

> *I just don't feel comfortable throwing away a decent man that I've known for 15 years in this time of complete chaos without there being a thorough investigation. So, I'm just sort of staying quiet about it.*

(Wray, 2020). All of a sudden, Milano found that "[t]he world is gray" when a friend is in the #MeToo crosshairs (Milano, 2020). Milano would write, "Believing women was never about 'Believe all women no matter what they say,' it was about changing the culture of NOT believing women by default" (Ibid.). She would tell Buzzfeed, "I think when we get into this place of believing women, regardless of giving men due process, it actually does more harm to the movement than good" (Felton, 2020). Certainly, Milano extends a concession to Biden that she willfully withheld from Kavanaugh. As Reade told *Fox News*, "[Milano] never reached out to me. I don't really want to amplify her voice because I feel like she hijacked my narrative for a while and framed it about herself" (Wulfsohn, 2020).

So much for the resoluteness of "I Believe Survivors."

Milano displayed her penchant for "agenda gymnastics," which left a bad taste in many mouths of the #MeToo movement as she provided cover for the left-leaning Biden that she denied the right-leaning Kavanaugh.

Milano's Buffoonish flip-flop drew the ire of her former co-star Rose McGowan, who had lived through her own #MeToo horrors and heroically led the charge to clean up Hollywood (Louszko, et. al., 2020). In a tweet directed squarely at Milano (McGowan, 2020), McGowan sought to expose Milano's progressive tribalism masked in faux activism:

> You are a fraud. This is about holding the media accountable. You go after Trump & Kavanaugh saying Believe Victims, you are a lie. You have always been a lie. The corrupt DNC is in on the smear job of Tara Reade, so are you. SHAME.

THE (SELF) MOCKERY OF REV. AL

One of my favorite movies is Brian De Palma's 1990 adaptation of Tom Wolfe's *The Bonfire of the Vanities*. Like many movies based on novels, De Palma took liberties with both the story and the characters. One such liberty was the portrayal of Reverend Bacon. Played by veteran actor John Hancock (no, not that one!), De Palma took "a canny, powerful, albeit crooked civic leader" in Wolfe's novel and turned Bacon into "a blustery buffoon sporting the velour running suit that is Sharpton's trademark" (Berkman, 1991).

Rev. Al did not take kindly to the portrayal, saying the film "makes a mockery out of me and the movement I represent" (Ibid.).

> *It's offensive to me that (the movie implies) I don't have enough sense to do the larceny myself. It's really degrading that Bacon lets a white guy use him.*

(Ibid.). Rev. Al rarely disappoints, right? If nothing else, the experience may have taught Sharpton a lesson in the power Hollywood wields in molding public perception.

That Rev. Al is a quick learner. A few years later, Rev. Al would self-own his bombastic reputation on the hit *ABC* series *Boston Legal* in an attempt to soften his image. Take this dialogue from a scene where Sharpton barges into a courtroom to deliver one of his infamous soliloquies, but has to shift the subject on the fly:

> *Al Sharpton: The image of Santa Claus has been crafted for hundreds, and hundreds, and hundreds of years. We're supposed to be in a different day. Give the world a black Santa Claus, let the people have an*

African-American come down the chimney bearing joy and good will!

Alan Shore: [whispers] Gay, not black.

Al Sharpton: The prejudice against gay people must stop. We all say we're for gay rights. We all say we accept homosexuality. But give a gay man a hug, sit in his lap?

(IMDb, 2021). Further perusal of Rev. Al's Internet Movie Database (IMDb) page reveals a list of self-deprecating and comical roles that he chose, an indication that Sharpton learned that playing the fool on the screen has more benefits than being portrayed by others as a real-life fool (Ibid.).

But alas, Hollywood fame is a double-edged sword. Every time Sharpton plays for laughs is a reminder of how ingrained into society's consciousness his decades of real-life Buffoonery has become.

Hollywood didn't soften Rev. Al; it confirmed who he is for all posterity: a perfect Buffoon.

CHAPTER 7

MERCENARY PENS AND MICS FOR HIRE: BUFFOONICUS AD-NEWSEAM

He chinks his purse, and takes his seat of state... And instant, fancy feels th' imputed sense.

It is reassuring to know that, even centuries ago, men of reason like Alexander Pope decried those talentless mercenaries in the media of his day who were writing on cue for the highest bidder (Breyfogle, 1999). It is equally terrifying to see how, even centuries ago, the same problems we see in media existed.

Today's "Grub Street" scribes (Tréguer, 2017) still indulge the rich and powerful, abandoning any pursuit of truth in favor of pursuing money and influence by indulging and enrapturing throngs through deceit and flattery. They are a class we call…

THE HACKS

The Hack stands on the periphery of politics. S/he rarely pursues elective office, never crafts any policy directly, and does not represent a ward or a district. Yet Hacks can hold more sway over who holds office and policy goals than many voting blocs because of their ability to sculpt and mold narratives intended to sway opinion under the guise of reporting facts. Thus, Hacks do not just report events; they create them.

By doing so, Hacks willingly disregard the journalist ethos by purposefully skewing their reporting in favor of a partisan view, which either they or their employer holds, in order to gain money and influence (not necessarily in that order). This practice of "yellow journalism" (or, if you prefer a less derogatory term, "the journalism of action" [Campbell, 2017]) is commonly associated with malpractice in newsgathering. Sensationalism, lies by omission, straw man arguments, increased hyperbole, and fact-shading are among the tools employed by Hacks in creating an "aesthetic fallacy" (Campbell, 2001)—a set of selected facts used to build into a "beautiful story" rather than facts functional to empirical truths (Fischer, 1970). In the midst of their crusade, Hacks paints themselves as heroic but actually, they are swindlers.

In this regard, the Hack's upward trajectory through our Sharpton Buffoonery MatrixTM tracks similarly to *Buffoonicus parasitos* in that the Hack's crusading ways may result in more frequent acts of Buffoonery carrying a higher BAM, triggering rapid BUN growth.

Since Hacks require favorable political outcomes to grow their influence and financial standing, every "beautiful story" plays out on a harsh, unscrupulous tribal battlefield of the twenty-four-hour news cycle. The Hack's need for increased money and influence creates the common narrative that every election is "the most important election of our time." That is, until the next election rolls around.

To improve their odds of gaining greater influence and increased finances, Hacks will seek greater access to newsmakers who share their like-minded partisan philosophy by ingratiating themselves through favorable coverage, which in turn builds their audience echo chamber. Of course, the newsmaker allows this because s/he benefits from the Hack's favorably shaded coverage. Conversely, Hacks are not above maligning newsmakers holding viewpoints in opposition to their personal or institutional interests to further satisfy the consumer's confirmation bias. Interestingly enough, those maligned newsmakers also allow this because they benefit from the sympathy engendered from the opposition consumer's confirmation bias within their own echo chamber. Thus, the Hack's avarice is significantly responsible for today's information bubbles dividing society and eroding civil discourse. It's a vicious cycle, as Hacks ultimately become slaves to their consumer's voracious consumption of content. As the pressure to keep feeding their self-created beasts builds, the Hack's already-biased work product often degrades, lacking proper foundation and becomes hastily gathered and communicated. The shortcuts become too much to maintain, especially as narratives change over time. As positions, or even employment, change, so must the Hack to maintain their money and influence.

A YELLOW JOURNALIST'S "FAKE NEWS" MYTH

One of the most popular quotes that feeds mistrust of the powerful and dangerous monolith that is mainstream news media comes from a famous telegram sent by William Randolph Hearst in response to his *New York Journal* correspondent in Cuba named Frederic Remington. As the story goes, Remington informed Hearst that he wished to return to New York because "[e]verything is quiet" in Cuba concerning growing tensions with Spain. The famed publisher asked Remington to "[p]lease remain. You furnish the pictures, and I'll furnish the war" (Campbell, 2017).

Many sources have since invoked Hearst's response to condemn the historical impact of mainstream media outlets exhibiting bias, including conservative columnist Charles Krauthammer in 2002.

Funny thing, though; the tale of Hearst's missive is most likely a myth that can be traced back to an unapologetic Hack named James Creelman.

Creelman was a "portly, bearded, cigar-chomping Canadian-born journalist prone to pomposity and exaggeration" who "relished making himself the hero of his own reporting" (Campbell, 2017). Long before referencing Hearst's telegram in his 1901 memoir, Creelman had developed a reputation among his peers for stretching the truth in his stories. Some have said he's gone as far as modifying direct quotes to say what he thought the interviewee wished to say (Dorwart, 1973).

You may notice similarities between Creelman's sort of journalism and today's mainstream press shaping the narrative

(Concha, 2021) for President Joe Biden or against President Donald Trump (Allsop & Vernon, 2020). This is just further proof that today's Buffoons are totally unoriginal.

While we take narrative shaping and media "personalities" as a given these days, the state of American journalism at the turn of the twentieth century was much different than it is today. As W. Joseph Campbell pointed out in 2017:

> *The ethos of fin-de-siécle American journalism was that a reporter has to 'sink his personality out of sight and merge his very identity in that of his paper.... . Every newspaper has a policy, determined by the editor-in-chief, and it is the reporter's duty to hew the line that has been stretched for him. Nobody cares what his private opinions may be upon matters political or things critical.'*

Thus, the fact that Creelman is even remembered as a Hack in a time when writers rarely received a byline (Campbell, 2017) makes Creelman's choice to "put so much of himself into an interview or story that the real subject of the article was utterly obscured" that much more significant in Buffoonish magnitude (BAM) (Abbot, 1933). It just was not done then.

Why Hearst indulged a Hack like Creelman stumped his contemporaries. As one columnist put it, "What an ass Creelman is…. I have often wondered whether Hearst supposes that anybody is fooled by his platitudinous nonsense" (*Journalist*, 1897). In actuality, Hearst's admiration for Creelman's zeal for taking on an assignment outweighed any concern for Creelman's lack of journalistic integrity (Ibid.). That trade-off notwithstanding, years before Creelman disclosed Hearst's quote in his memoir, his contemporaries found good reason to question Creelman's faithfulness to truth in reporting.

For example, in 1894, Creelman filed reports to the *New York World* claiming that Japanese soldiers were slaughtering Chinese civilians at Port Arthur during the Sino-Japanese War (Dorwart, 1973). Creelman's accounts were horrifying, but also roundly dismissed. The *New York Tribune* declared Creelman's story "so untrue that to call them wild exaggerations would be gross flattery" (New York Tribune, 1894). Edwin Dun, the US minister to Japan, confirmed as much, concluding after a thorough investigation into Creelman's claims that "the account sent to 'The World' by Mr. Creelman is sensational in the extreme and a gross exaggeration of what occurred" (National Archives, 1894).

Ouch.

Later, in 1898, Creelman wrote another sensationalized claim of how he single-handedly captured Spanish soldiers during a battle at El Caney in Cuba while taking a bullet to his left shoulder to boot (Campbell, 2017). Creelman's astonishing first-person account tells how "[he] went up to the [Spanish] officer, and looking him straight in the eye, said in French: 'You are my prisoner'" and how, in response, the officer "threw up his hands and said, 'Do with me as you please'" (Ibid.)

Brian Williams wept! (Farhi, 2015).

Again, Creelman's colleagues mocked "Port Arthur Creelman" for this latest improbable misadventure:

> When [Creelman] really gets his blood up, what he wants to do is to surround and capture armies, to fly into the imminently deadly breach, to beat back regiments with his single sword, and to scale the dizziest heights in quest of glory.... But not everyone could have charged up that hill... intimidated those Spaniards crouching there.... That's what Creelman did, however; he tells us so himself.

(Campbell, 2017). Such was Creelman's credibility, which provides the proper context to examine Hearst's reply to Remington.

Scholars much smarter than me have determined the many reasons why Hearst's now-famous line is likely another Creelman fabrication. First, Creelman was in Europe when Hearst purportedly transmitted it (Ibid.), meaning Creelman had no first-hand knowledge of any such telegram. Also, Creelman inaccurately stated in his memoir that the correspondent receiving Hearst's telegram, Frederic Remington, was stuck in Cuba "until the war began" (Creelman, 1901) when he had only been hired for a month (Campbell, 2017). In fact, Remington did not remain in Cuba as Hearst requested, but instead left Cuba after six days (Ibid.). When Remington returned, his illustrations from Cuba did not reveal that "everything is quiet." Quite the contrary, Remington depicted great unrest in Cuba (Ibid.).

So how did Creelman's "fake news" become so commonly referenced? Why, Hollywood, of course! *Citizen Kane*, that masterpiece of cinema loosely based on Hearst's life, featured a similar quotation from Orson Welles, vowing, "You provide the prose poems, and I'll provide the war." And with that, journalism changed. Welles transformed a line that Creelman originally intended as a throw-away compliment to Hearst into more of a threat.

To Creelman, "providing the war" was never sinister, it was his job:

> How little they know of yellow journalism who denounce it! How swift they are to condemn its shrieking headlines, its exaggerated pictures, its coarse buffoonery, its intrusions upon private life, and its occasional inaccuracies! But how slow they are to see the steadfast guardianship of public interests which it maintains! How blind to its unfearing warfare against rascality, its detection and prosecution of crime, its costly searchings for knowledge throughout the earth, its exposures of humbug, its endless funds for the quick relief of distress!

(Creelman, 1901). Is this not the quintessential embodiment of "aesthetic fallacy"? There can be no clearer example that, for Hacks like Creelman, journalistic ethics just get in the way of their beautiful story. Facts be damned.

THE SELF-IMPORTANT CELEBRITY JOURNALIST

Today's modern media landscape resembles the yellow journalism of Creelman's day. This is especially true as it pertains to the twenty-four-hour national cable news networks that mix news coverage with commentary and "politi-tainment" from pundits and personalities blurring the line between news and narrative.

Among those in today's media who would seemingly fall in line with Creelman's philosophy of journalism is *CNN*'s chief White House correspondent, Jim Acosta. In his 2020 book, *The Enemy of the People: A Dangerous Time to Tell the Truth in America*, Acosta responded to accusations that his coverage of President Donald Trump was biased by proclaiming, "Neutrality for the sake of neutrality doesn't really serve us in the age of Trump."

Acosta's Buffoonery came into hyper-focus during his coverage of the Trump administration starting in the fall of 2015. From the start, Acosta apparently felt offended, and even a little threatened, by Trump's political posture and subsequent success in 2016:

> I'll never forget what I saw on the campaign trail and what I have witnessed covering the Trump presidency. Even now, more than two years into his presidency, it's still shocking to remember Trump, as a presidential candidate, saying he could stand in the middle of Fifth Avenue and shoot somebody and get away with it. It's still shocking to remember him... describing Mexican undocumented immigrants as "rapists -and still escaping the kind of accountability that would have knocked anyone else out of the race.

(Acosta, 2020). Having been raised in a household of first- and second-generation Italian Americans, I know a vendetta when I see one. In January of 2017, after *CNN* had picked up *Buzzfeed*'s infamously inaccurate story about a Russian dossier containing salacious and unverified claims (Cullison and Volz, 2019), the President-elect refused to take a question from Acosta, calling his network "fake news" (Sutton, 2017).

From there, it was game on.

Virtually every report Acosta filed from the Trump White House was a hodge-podge mixture of news reporting and personal commentary. Whether filing a daily report, or even amid a daily press briefing, Acosta would, admittedly, grandstand and showboat, writing that he "opts for the bait"

(Wulfsohn, May 2019). In doing so, Acosta not only became a prime target for President Trump's often antagonistic relationship with mainstream media, but a distraction among his colleagues who say that Acosta's reporting "doesn't always need to be about him and his grandstanding. People get tired of it. Acosta is supposed to be a correspondent reporting the facts, but you can't tell the difference between him and a paid pundit" (Ibid.). Acosta became less like a reporter and more like a rival demanding equal time.

It looks like we have the makings of a modern-day James Creelman. The comparison holds up when examining the integrity (or lack thereof) of some of Acosta's reporting.

In June of 2018, Acosta took to social media to claim that President Trump did not respond to his question of where he would stop calling the mainstream media the "enemy of the people" (Acosta, 2018). However, a video of that moment posted online thereafter shows Acosta standing in the back of a room, screaming the question over loud applause, calling into question whether President Trump even heard Acosta's attempt at grandstanding from so far away (Levine, 2018).

In February of 2019, after a summit with North Korean dictator Kim Jong-un, President Trump took questions from the world media but failed to call on Acosta. At the end of the press conference, Acosta went on air to lament his plight and claimed that Trump "steered clear largely" of himself and the White House press corps "by design" (Nolte, 2019). According to the Media Research Center, Acosta seemingly lied by omission, as Trump had called on at least six members of the White House press corps (Houck, 2019).

In May of 2019, Acosta claimed on social media that President Trump accused asylum seekers of making "frivolous claims" as proof of Trump's malign view toward immigration (Acosta, 2019). President Trump's actual quote was that "[u]nfortunately legitimate asylum seekers are being displaced by those lodging frivolous claims," thus presenting a more nuanced position than Acosta led his followers to believe (Spiering, 2019).

But I've saved the best for last. In November of 2018, according to seasoned journalist Frank Miele, Acosta "gave President Trump a moral lecture in the form of a loaded 'question' about why Trump called the migrant 'caravan' an 'invasion.' According to Acosta, it is not an invasion because the migrants were hundreds of miles away, and besides, the migrants aren't going to be 'climbing over walls and so on'" (Miele, 2018). A week later, the so-called "caravan" was "sitting astride the border wall and invading US territory" (Ibid.). This battle of semantics soon turned ugly. Acosta refused to pass a microphone to another reporter when Trump directed him to do so, prompting a female intern to attempt to take it from Acosta, who used his arms to block her.

As Frank Miele further observed, Acosta's true Buffoonery was not his argument; it was his self-importance:

> Pardon me for not joining the journalistic pack and defending the divine right of reporters to act as buffoonishly as possible without suffering consequences. I know that is the response de rigueur for editors when someone like Acosta goes out of bounds, but I bring nearly four decades of experience in community

> journalism to the table, and to me Acosta is just one more self-important reporter who gives a bad name to the hard-working journalists who take their job more seriously than their haircut.

(Ibid.). Acosta's seemingly willful inaccuracies and theatrics are reminiscent of Creelman's "journalism of action." In Acosta's case, his "beautiful story" portrays himself as a crusader for truth against a president who doesn't know the meaning of the word.

Like Creelman, Acosta intends to cement his image as a fighter for freedom of the press and, therefore, of the people. But Acosta is more like a grifter out to make himself and his network more marketable and thus, richer. That is why Acosta wrote his memoir: to parlay his visibility and his narcissistic self-image into bank. Unfortunately for him, Acosta's book was largely a flop (Wulfsohn, June 2019):

> Acosta used it as an opportunity to relitigate his spats with the White House rather than to meaningfully interrogate the cultural shift that left huge numbers of people despising and fearing the press.

(Quinn, 2019). And so, the comparison to Creelman comes full circle: Jim Acosta is, in every sense, a modern-day Hack who may not have been an "enemy of the people" in the age of Trump, but he surely was no friend, either.

As the title above indicates (Stiles, 2014), no one would mistake Rev. Al for a news journalist. But as discussed earlier, his misadventures as the host of a show on *MSNBC* certainly qualifies him as a member of the mainstream media. Back before his show was cast into the recesses of weekend viewing, Rev. Al received heavy criticism for his biased news agenda, including surprising indictments from progressives.

Imagine my shock in finding none other than far-left professor Cornel West leveling attacks on Rev. Al's media cred. "Al Sharpton is who?" declared West, calling him "a cheerleader for Obama."

> "*MSNBC*, state press, it's all Obama propaganda. And Sharpton is the worst."

(Ibid.). Professor West's point is well taken, especially given that months before Sharpton took the gig at *MSNBC*, *CBS*'s *60 Minutes* reported that "Sharpton told us that having a black president is a challenge: if he finds fault with Mr. Obama, he'd be aiding those who want to destroy him. So he has decided not to criticize the president about…" (CBS News, 2011). For a would-be journalist/pundit to make such a promise is concerning to say the least, as a real journalist, Glenn Greenwald, so aptly explains:

> How can a media outlet such as MSNBC that purports to be presenting political journalism possibly employ someone as a journalist—even an opinion journalist—who publicly and categorically pledges never to criticize the President of the United States under any circumstances? That would be like hiring a physician who vows never to treat any diseases, or employing an auto mechanic who pledges never to fix any cars, or retaining a pollster who swears never to make any findings about public opinion. Holding people in political power accountable is the prime function—the defining feature—of a journalist, including a pundit; if you expressly and publicly vow never to do that, how can you possibly be credibly presented as being one? And how can the political analysis of someone who takes this pledge possibly be trusted as sincerely held, let alone accurate?

(Greenwald, 2011). The answer is that you can't trust someone like Rev. Al Sharpton.

CHAPTER 8

PUSHING BEYOND THE ENVELOPE: BUFFOONICUS AMBITIOUS

From the first tales of Icarus with his waxed wings flying too close to the sun, to the present-day falls from grace that occur all too often, history is littered with countless cautionary tales of the inexorable connection between power and corruption succinctly summarized by John Emerich Edward Dalberg-Acton, First Baron Acton, that "[p]ower tends to corrupt, and absolute power corrupts absolutely" (Figgis, 1907).

Over a century later, essayist Ken Ringle took his own deep dive in the *Washington Post* to explain why we "mortals who, finding themselves garbed in the unaccustomed robes of leadership or success, start imagining themselves bulletproofed against disaster—and so tempt the fates."

Taking our cues from Lord Acton, Ringle, and even Icarus himself, let's focus on a Political Buffoon with such a rapacious appetite for power that she/he corrupts an otherwise promising political career. We will call them...

THE EGOTISTS

This classification of Buffoon exhibits a profoundly exaggerated sense of self-importance borne from some recognition of his/her political talents. As University of South Carolina Betty Glad once astutely observed, Egotists "gain power in part because they're smart or clever, and then start believing they're smarter and cleverer than anyone" (Ringle, 1998). Former New York Governor Eliot Spitzer, who once famously claimed to be "a fucking steamroller" ready to "roll over you or anybody else" immediately springs to mind (Reuters, 2007). We all know what happened to Spitzer, also known as "Client No. 9," and his "fucking steamroller" once he got caught up in an investigation into a high-class prostitution ring (Feuer & Urbina, 2008).

This brings us to the next identifying characteristic: Egotists lose sight of their personal and professional limitations and embrace increasing riskier political calculations. To borrow further from Ringle, Egotists "convince themselves there's really no risk in their fatal attraction to the spinning prop. How could there be when they're smarter, luckier, craftier, and uniquely blessed by both God and destiny?" (Ibid.). Inherent in the Egotist's overestimation of themselves is, as Professor Glad further observes, a corresponding underestimation of the talents and capabilities of others (Ringle,

1998)—especially those who eventually bring the Egotist crashing down.

In this sense, the Egotist is an order of magnitude greater than *Buffoonicus oblivious*: the Narcissist. Both the Narcissist and the Egotist are blinded by their delusions of omnipotence and dazzled by their own perceived invincibility. But the two are starkly different. First, a Narcissist is often less talented politically than the Egotist, as the latter finds comparatively greater political success in a short time thanks to their skill, while the former relies more on self-image rather than skill for whatever mediocre success they achieve.

Since the Egotist actually has some education, skill, or talent, our Sharpton Buffoonery MatrixTM is less forgiving, with each act of Buffoonery carrying a significantly higher BAM (and in turn, rapid growth in BUN) than a lesser hypocrite like *Buffoonicus oblivious*. The reason, simply put: The Egotist should know better.

Another starker difference between the two lies in the Egotist's ravenous search for their next rush of adrenaline (Ibid.). Power and influence fuels the Egotist's "need for speed"; the more fuel injected into the engine, the faster it burns, and the faster the Egotist flies down his political track. But with greater speed comes greater danger and, eventually, the Egotist will hit reality like a wall at the brickyard.

A "MORAL BLIND SPOT" FELLS A GIANT IN THE MAKING

Edward F. Prichard Jr. may be the most talented politician you've never heard of.

The scion of a successful horse breeder from Kentucky (New York Times, 1984), Pritchard was a prodigy with a photographic memory (Campbell, 2010). He entered Princeton at sixteen, graduating at the top of his class. He graduated Harvard Law School *magna cum laude*, and by twenty-four, was law clerk to his mentor, Supreme Court Justice Felix Frankfurter (New York Times, 1949). Prichard later served in various capacities on the staff of two presidents (Ibid.) including FDR, who counted Prichard, now thirty, among his "brain trust" of the New Deal (Harwood, 1984). Those who knew him believed Prichard was destined to hold the highest office in the world. He was, as Arthur Schlesinger, Jr. remembered, "a man of dazzling brilliance" (Ibid.).

So why is it that only real history buffs recognize his name? Because baked into Prichard's talent was an air of superiority and invincibility that caused him to make poor decisions. For example, during his political upbringing, Prichard "manipulated student elections, read other people's mail, and acted as if the ethical rules that applied to others were not for him" (Gould, 1999). It was a taste of things to come.

When Prichard started charting his own political path, he turned his as-of-yet unchecked impulses toward the 1948 election (New York Times, 1949). It was rumored that either Prichard or his father had laid a sizeable wager on what the margin of the Democratic majority would be in his county

(Campbell, 2010). To ensure that he won (the wager, that is), Prichard forged signatures on over two hundred ballots and stuffed the boxes before the polls opened (New York Times, 1949). Amazingly, Prichard saw his crime as no big deal. After all, "my father did it, my great-grandfather did it" (Campbell, 2010). So why shouldn't he be just as immune from punishment as they were?

But unlike his forefathers, Prichard was charged with a crime and convicted after Judge W.B. Ardery, his former law school roommate, testified that Prichard admitted his prank to him privately (Ibid.). Prichard would be sentenced to two years in prison, of which he only served five months, thanks to a presidential pardon from President Truman (Harwood, 1984).

How silly it must have been for the invincible Prichard to have been brought down for partaking in a stupid tradition by a friend's betrayal of confidence. For a man of such talent, Prichard's explanation for his actions was incredibly naïve:

> *I was raised to believe that (monkeying with elections) was just second nature. There I was on the one hand with all those great and moral and intellectual principles, believing I ought to stand for the good, the true and the beautiful; and on the other hand thinking it's perfectly all right to stuff a ballot box. Now that's an absolute dichotomy, but that's the kind of dichotomy I got into, and it's absolutely unforgivable.*

(Pearce, 1983). But why, Edward, why? Prichard never confirmed the rumor about the wager, only saying, "I thought of it as something you did for fun. It was sort of a moral blind spot" (Harwood, 1984).

Ya think?

It took decades for Prichard to recover from his humbling experience, but he eventually found some measure of redemption in his later life. Prichard offered valued counsel to many office holders and served on commissions and such (Ibid.). But he never reached the dizzying heights that many felt he was destined to reach.

A HUCKSTER, ENABLED BY MEDIA, FALLS PRECIPITOUSLY

From the beginning of the Trump presidency, an embattled corporate media looked for a hero—the anti-Trump, if you will, who could beat him at his own game.

Enter Michael Avenatti, a brash California attorney with a penchant for racing cars (Shilling, 2018) who, by all indications, made a good living as a litigator to famous

Hollywood-types like Paris Hilton (Page Six, 2007) and Christina Aguilera (Farache, 2000). He had even sued Trump before he was president (Niemietz, 2018).

After some moderate success (Los Angeles Times, 2017) and a taste of national media attention (Cooper, 2016), Avenatti's national profile truly took off in 2016 when he represented a porn star named Stormy Daniels (real name Stephanie Clifford) who sought to nullify a non-disclosure agreement where, allegedly, she had been paid hush money to keep news of a twelve-year extramarital affair with now-President Trump quiet (Dunleavy, 2021). With his "basta" catchphrase (Ibid.) and his ballsy approach in confronting all things Trump, Avenatti became a hit among the "resistance" of lefty Twitter, which helped him reach folk-hero status very quickly. Meanwhile, his slimy nature combined with his representation of Daniels earned Avenatti the now-infamous title of "creepy porn lawyer" from critics on the right (Bever, 2018).

Corporate media immediately picked up Avenatti's scent, and the two immediately engaged in a mutually beneficial relationship. Anti-Trump media featured Avenatti, sometimes more than once per day, as someone who *finally* will *really* take down Trump. Avenatti, in turn, peddled his caustic brand of hope-pium to their swooning masses (Taibbi, 2019). All told, Avenatti made 254 appearances on major news networks in 2018, including 122 appearances on *CNN*. (D'Agostino, 2019). That includes a ten-week span of 147 Avenatti interviews, with *CNN* conducting more than half of them (D'Agostino, et. al., 2018).

Mikey liked it.

CNN's contributors fell particularly hard for Avenatti. For Chrissakes, *CNN*'s Ana Navarro compared Avenatti to the "Holy Spirit" (Taibbi, 2019). None fell harder than Brian Stelter, who told Avenatti on his show *Reliable Sources* that he was "taking him serious[ly]" as a presidential contender (Luciano, 2021).[6]

Riding high, Avenatti filed a defamation suit in May of 2018 against President Trump for claiming in a tweet that Daniels's initial accusations were a "total con job" (Fitzpatrick & Connor, 2018). Within five months, a federal judge dismissed Daniels's defamation suit (Sullivan, 2018). A few months after that, another federal judge threw Daniels's NDA-nullification case in the same legal trash bin (Baker, 2019). Looking back, that lawsuit might have been the moment where it all unraveled for Avenatti.

Avenatti persisted, albeit just as poorly, inserting himself into confirmation hearings for now-Supreme Court Justice Brett Kavanaugh. Avenatti represented Julie Swetnick, who accused Kavanaugh of gang rape (Damron, 2018). Many found Swetnick's accusations less than credible (Ibid.); the Senate referred both Swetnick and Avenatti to the Department of Justice for a criminal probe into her "materially false" statements (Kim, 2018).

Now zero-for-two in big-time politics, Avenatti launched an ill-fated campaign to challenge President Trump in November of 2018 (Korecki, 2018). A month later, Avenatti shut it

---

6   Just as a side note, if there is a more ironic title for a show, I haven't found it yet; Stelter is a Hack of the first degree.

down (Mangan, 2018). That probably had something to do his mounting legal troubles. Shortly after launching his first campaign ad, Avenatti was arrested on suspicion of domestic violence (Sykes, 2018).

Yet Avenatti's climatic crash was still to come. In March of 2019, federal prosecutors in New York charged that Avenatti attempted to extort millions from Nike (Davis O'Brien, et. al., 2019). A month later, federal prosecutors in California charged Avenatti with a laundry list of criminality concerning millions he allegedly embezzled from a paraplegic client (US Dept. of Justice, 2019). Jail time followed (NPR, 2021). Another federal conviction followed; this time for embezzling funds from his former meal ticket Daniels (Mangan, 2022).

A little over a year after the comparisons to God, Avenatti's fifteen minutes were up, leaving those in media who fell for his hustle regretting all those snapshots taken alongside him in the Hamptons (Ibid.).

These days, Avenatti, is "most fearful of the fact that the rate of descent is greater than the rate of ascent. Some would argue at this point that I flew too close to the sun. As I sit here today, yes, absolutely, I know I did. No question. Icarus" (Fox, 2020).

You're not Icarus, Mike. You're just another twenty-first-century snake oil salesman.

THERE CAN BE ONLY ONE!

We've discussed Rev. Al's ambitions before: that while he is *a* voice of Black America, he craves being *the* voice of Black America. Whether it be his run for president or his love for the limelight, Rev. Al's goal has been to carry that mantle, which most of his peers agreed has long been carried by Rev. Jesse Jackson.

The first signs of trouble brewing between "Big Rev" Jackson and "Little Rev" Sharpton came in 2000 when they each took opposing sides in a franchise dispute between Burger King and a Black franchisee named La-Van Hawkins. Sharpton sided with Hawkins, while Jackson stood with Burger King, whom he had partnered with on his "Wall Street Project" (Newfield, 2002). This was one of many clashes between Sharpton and Jackson, but it signaled a significant divergence in their respective philosophies:

> Sharpton's vast ambition has never exactly been a secret. And Jackson's focus on corporate America—what some have called the velvet shakedown—has taken him away from his protest roots toward Wall Street and Silicon Valley, leaving Sharpton an opening.

(Ibid.). The relationship went downhill from there.

The strongest indication that Sharpton was gunning for Jackson's "spot" came during an appearance on Fox News in 2001. In a jailhouse interview, Rev. Al deflected his role in the Tawana Brawley case by comparing it to a longstanding Jackson controversy. "I think the Brawley case pales in comparison," Sharpton said (Ibid.). "Did I take the blood of the guy I loved and put it on my shirt?" (Ortega, 2001).

If you don't know the reference, Sharpton was referring to a past controversy where some had said that Jackson, who was present when Rev. Martin Luther King, Jr. was assassinated, tried to score political points by smearing Rev. King's blood on his clothes (Anderson and Spear, 1987). Many leaders of the time questioned whether it was even Dr. King's blood at all (Ibid.).

Ew.

Sharpton's sharp retort did not sit well with many Black leaders, including a "very disappointed" Rep. Charles Rangel (D-NY) (Ortega, 2001). Even Donna Brazile, who was Al Gore's former presidential campaign manager at the time, came to Jackson's defense (Newfield, 2002).

Sharpton would later try to cover his rear end by saying the media misinterpreted him, insisting that he raised the claim to show how the media was discrediting him much like they attempted to do to Rev. Jackson (Ortega, 2001). But the damage caused by his ambition had been done. Eventually, Rev. Al would publicly apologize to Rev. Jesse, which seemed more like crisis management than real contrition; that would come years later. Sharpton recounted how he apologized to Jackson for letting his pursuit of power get the better of him:

> *I realized that personal ambition had a lot to do with motivating my disagreements with him. Somewhere along the way, the student gets the misconception that your rise is dependent on the moving on of the teacher, and it has nothing to do with that. He'd invested a lot in me, and believed in me before anyone thought I'd be viable, and it was wrong for me to feel that my ambition was more important than our relationship.*

(Hedegaard, 2004).

See? Even Rev. Al can learn from his Buffoonery.

PART III

THE IRREDEEMABLES

CHAPTER 9

THE TIPPING POINT: BUFFOONICUS SOPHISTRIUS

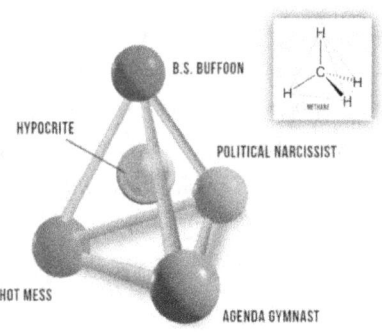

The Lesser Hypocrites Tetrahedron: Note that its structure is similar to methane, which is commonly found in flatulence.

Up until now, we have been able to poke fun at the Buffoons of lesser magnitude whom we have examined. But we must now recognize that each acts as a gateway to a less humorous and more dangerous Buffoon variant. One could argue that each Lesser Hypocrite variant discussed thus far—the "BS" Buffoon, the Hot Mess, the Agenda Gymnast, and the

Political Narcissist—are each a specialized, albeit lesser, rendition of this next Buffoon. Each can intersect greatly with each other; thus, each Lesser Hypocrite studied thus far can be considered a "hybrid" possessing two or more sets of the traits of one type.

All roads have led us to this examination of what happens when a lesser hypocrite is left unchecked or undeterred. They become...

THE HYPOCRITE

Instead of offering my baseline definition for this variation of political Buffoon, I gladly defer to the great Benjamin Franklin to begin our discussion:

> *[A] publick Hypocrite every day deceives his betters, and makes them the Ignorant Trumpeters of his supposed Godliness: They take him for a Saint, and pass him for one, without considering that they are (as it were) the Instruments of publick Mischief out of Conscience, and ruin their Country for God's sake.*

("Silence Dogood", 1722). The Hypocrite is too far gone. Their cognitive dissonance, derived from whatever gateway Buffoonery has been left unchecked for so long, is completely ingrained in the Hypocrite's personal and political identity. The Hypocrite has crossed the dividing line from the rather benign variants of Buffoon into hypocrisy so many times that they developed a callous and unrepentant disposition.

The Hypocrite has no need to relieve any internal tension created by the inconsistency of their words and actions because they simply don't care anymore and therefore revel in the freedom from such bounds. This is an important distinction that distills our definition of hypocrisy beyond the common everyday usage of the word. The more benign Buffoons discussed in previous chapters may act unconsciously in a hypocritical way but recognize their Buffoonery and probably still care enough to feel contrite. Moreover, one may act like a hypocrite and simply be a troubled individual who recognizes right from wrong but nonetheless possesses a compulsion toward the latter.

While both have acted hypocritically, neither is *the* Hypocrite. It is not hyperbole to say that Hypocrites are left unchecked and allowed to increase in number; they pose an existential threat to American society:

> *When ordinary political campaigns consist, as they recently have, of candidates calling one another liars, it is hard to make the case to the next generation that honesty is the prime virtue in public life and that a few pitiable wretches are too weak to observe its strictures. It is much more likely for children to grow up believing that it is all a game, that the rules exist only for display and that anybody is free to break them.*

(Ehrenhalt, 2001). This is precisely the great challenge of our time: to understand, suppress, and ultimately, eradicate the Hypocrite from American political culture.

How the Hypocrite arrives at this advanced stage of Buffoonery can vary. One way is to ignore a lesser Buffoon to the point where she/he has never felt the need to justify past unreasonable actions. Alternatively, a lesser Buffoon might be called out, but is too ignorant, arrogant, or some combination of both to acknowledge the need to change. Needless to say, the Hypocrite, by its very nature, overshadows any lesser Buffoon already discussed in terms of both BUN and BAM on our Sharpton Buffoonery MatrixTM.

Regardless, within the psyche of the Hypocrite, morality, pragmatism, and sensibility have been subverted by greed, hubris, and the need to gain and maintain power.

They truly make the world a lesser place for the multitudes they purport to serve.

GO HOME, CONGRESSMAN. YOU'RE DRUNK

Upon taking office, an elected official takes an oath to, among other things, support and defend the Constitution. I know it sounds corny, but it's a pretty big deal. The Hypocrite disregards the gravity and importance of their pledge; it is merely a means to their end.

You may not realize this, but many in government fail to practice what they pass. I know. I'm shocked, too.

The Prohibition Era was an age of hypocrisy where many members of Congress seemingly stuffed their oath and their principles somewhere in the back of their liquor cabinet. Let's set the stage to show why Prohibition gave us the best examples of political hypocrisy.

THE FIRST LADY OF THE LAW SPILLS THE TEA
Even after the Eighteenth Amendment outlawed the production and shipment of intoxicating beverages and the Volstead Act introduced legislation to enforce its provisions (thanks, Republicans), debate on Prohibition split Congress into proponents and opponents labeled "Drys" and "Wets" (US House of Representatives, 2019). The label may have matched an official's political position taken, but when it came to the "Drys," it didn't necessarily match their behavior.

We know about Prohibition hypocrisy because Mabel Walker Willebrandt, a former US Assistant Attorney General in charge of Prohibition cases, so thoroughly exposed this point (Kratz, 2021). Willebrandt was a pioneering badass buster of Buffoons for whom we Buffoonologists owe a great debt of gratitude. Though she was no fan of Prohibition (Ibid.), Willebrandt shared her knowledge of "Senators and Representatives… on the floor of the Senate and House in a drunken condition" (Ibid.) in nationally published articles (Willebrandt, 1929). One such article told of an un-named Senator who "objected to and prevented legislation while in such a condition of intoxication that he had to hold to his desk to keep himself upright" (US House of Representatives, 2019).

If only C-SPAN were around then.

Willebrandt also told her readers how "[b]ootleggers infest the halls and corridors of Congress and ply their trade there" (Willebrandt, 1929). No wonder Willebrandt was so clearly disgusted:

> *I think that probably nothing has done more to disgust and alienate honest men and women who originally strongly favored the prohibition amendment and its strict enforcement than the hypocrisy of the wet-drinking, dry-voting Congressmen.*
>
> *I have found, however, a curious impression or state of mind among members of Congress... that they are above and beyond... the law. Their attitude would be amusing if it were not so tragic in its effect upon the great mass of people who abhor the hypocrisy manifested by these dry-wet officials.*

(Ibid.). See what I mean about Willebrandt being a badass buster of Buffoons? Willebrandt captured the quintessential hypocrisy of her time: these "wet-drinking, dry-voting Congressmen" and their serious breaches of the public's trust.

Yet with all the tea spillage, Willebrandt never named names.

But I will.

THE "LEAKY TRUNK" CONGRESSMEN

In January of 1929, an employee of the American Railway Express company called the office of the Prohibition Administration for Washington, DC, to report a "leaking suitcase" at Union Station that "smells like liquor" (New York Times,

November 20, 1929). Prohibition Enforcement Service agents responded and confirmed the call. When agent Basil Quinn opened the leaky suitcase, he found that it contained "six broken bottles and six unbroken bottles of 'assorted' liquors," thus solving the source of both the leak and the smell (Ibid.). The reporting employee later told Quinn that the leaky suitcase was part of a larger shipment that included a trunk that had already been shipped to the same address written on the wet suitcase: Room 411 of what is now the Cannon House Office Building (Ibid.).

But that couldn't be because that was the office of Congressman Edward Denison (R-IL) (US House of Representatives, 2021), who was known to be "about the last person those on Capitol Hill expected to run afoul the District bone-dry net" (New York Times, November 20, 1929). After all, the Illinois congressman had voted for every prohibition bill that came across his desk (US House of Representatives, 2019).

The leaky suitcase aroused suspicion: What else was shipped to Denison's office? Denison told Quinn and his agents that the trunk contained a set of dishes he had bought in Panama while on official business in the Canal Zone. Unimpressed by Denison's explanation, Quinn and his inspectors compelled the congressman to produce the trunk and to open it (New York Times, November 20, 1929). Denison couldn't produce a key for the trunk initially, and when he did later that evening, it did not work. Denison then claimed the trunk wasn't his, pointing to the name "B.B. Dawson" written on it as proof (Ibid.). The inspectors, having noted that the name was not there earlier, weren't having it, so they broke it open and found another "eighteen bottles of real Scotch whisky and a half a dozen bottles of gin labeled 'Dilboy'" neatly packed therein (Ibid.).

The jig was up, see.

Or was it? Willebrandt indicted Denison for possessing intoxicating liquor in violation of the National Prohibition Act, but a jury found Denison not guilty despite a "fairy story" defense of switched luggage, painted-on names, disappeared keys, incompetence shippers and a vast conspiracy by inspectors (US v. Denison). Hats off to Denison's lawyer; that's one helleva job!

One question remained: How did Denison's liquor get into the country in the first place? As I mentioned, Denison claimed to have just returned from Panama, a "wet" nation. At this time, the Department of Treasury would grant members of Congress returning from abroad "freedom of the port" (Willebrandt, 1929). This meant their luggage passed without inspection upon their return from their "official mission," or vacation junket (Time, April 1929).

After all, customs checks are for the little people.

In response, Congress passed the Jones Act, which stiffened penalties for all prohibition-related offenses to five years in the pokey and a ten-thousand-dollar fine (the equivalent of $160,000 in today's dollars. Man, inflation sucks!). Ironically, Denison voted in favor of the Jones Act, as did William M. Morgan (R-OH) and M. Alfred Michaelson (R-IL) (New York Times, March 30, 1929).

Morgan's district in the Buckeye State was said to be "drier than burnt toast" (Okrent, 2010)—the driest district in the driest state in the Union. (New York Times, March 30, 1929). So imagine his constituency's shock at news that prohibition inspectors found four bottles of whisky in one of Morgan's bags upon returning to the Port of New York from Panama after "official business" trips abroad (Ibid.). But he wasn't. Morgan's colleague, Rep. Fiorello LaGuardia (R-NY), had already informed officials that he and about fourteen other representatives had taken a personal trip to Panama where he honeymooned with his wife (Ibid.). His supporters would have been doubly shocked to learn Morgan attempted to claim "free entry" while his inspectors started opening his bags, probably to conceal his wrongdoing. As if that weren't enough, those same poor constituents would have swooned to hear that Morgan not only admitted during the inspection to have imported the liquor, but that he pulled a Karen-esque, "Don't you know who I am?" tirade, exclaiming, "Who is this man [the inspector]? I'll take care of him when I get to Washington" (Ibid.).

Morgan later claims the booze was a gift for his father-in-law, a Civil War veteran, but even that story fell apart when the elder Mr. Morgan told a reporter, "If there was any liquor brought for me, I haven't seen any of it around here" (Okrent, 2010).

Gotta love in-laws.

Morgan's tale of woe hit the papers just as the ink dried, and here's comes Michaelson, another staunch "dry" man (New

York Times, March 29, 1929) despite second-hand political connections to Al Capone himself (Grossman, 2008). Like Morgan, he claimed "free entry" upon his return home from Cuba (New York Times, March 29, 1929) and would've gotten away with it when, according to his indictment, one of his bags sprang a leak (Okrent, 2010). Michaelson's cache, in comparison to Denison and Morgan, was much more exotic:

> *According to the indictment, one of Michaelson's trunks contained six quarts of whiskey, two of creme de menthe, one each of several other liqueurs, and a whole keg of something the indictment identified as "plum barbacourt," which was almost certainly Rhum Barbancourt, from Haiti.*

(Grossman, 2010). Also like Morgan, Michaelson passed the buck onto an in-law (Okrent, 2010). But unlike Morgan, Michaelson's brother-in-law, Walter Gramm, took the bullet and pled guilty (Time, November 1929). The presiding judge was less than pleased:

> *"He was a 'fall guy,'" frankly explained Gramm's lawyer.*
>
> *Said the judge: "I have no desire to punish him for the faults of the escaped Congressman—one of those who votes dry and drinks wet."*

(Ibid.). Gramm got off with a one-thousand-dollar fine (Ibid.).

The judge's stomach for hypocrisy was far less tolerant than Michaelson's colleagues in the Republican majority in Congress, the Chair of the House Rules Committees, Rep.

Bertrand Snell (R-NY), barely batted an eye, calling news of Michaelson's indictment "a rather unimportant matter" (New York Times. March 30, 1929). Further proof that anyone who tells you that partisan tribalism is a modern convention does not know American history.

FREDO'S FUGAZY COVID-19(84) PIETY

When the COVID-19 pandemic changed the rules of everyday living to such an extreme degree, it served as fertile ground for exposing Hypocrites who feel that lockdowns and masking are for everyone but them.

Chris Cuomo, also known as "Fredo," is one such person.

Before we begin, let's establish some proper nomenclature. From this point on, I will be referring to Chris Cuomo as "Fredo" (Gold, 2019). But it is not meant as a slur against his Italian American heritage, which I share. In the past, "Fredo" has threatened to "throw [a man] down [a flight of] stairs" and "f---ing ruin [his] s—t" (Creitz, 2020) because "Fredo" equates his name with the N-word (Wilkinson, 2019). That's a wide exaggeration to this Italian American, as I have always associated the term "Fredo" not as an ethnic slur, but as slang for, as "Fredo" himself put it, "the weak brother" (Gold, 2019), à *la* the tragically weak Fredo Corleone of Mario Puzo's *The Godfather*. So let's be clear: When I refer to "Fredo," it has nothing to do with his race or ethnicity. It has everything to do with my informed opinion that "Fredo" is a weak-minded Hypocrite, with my reasoning to follow.

We all knew the drill for preventing the spread of COVID-19 in the spring of 2020. Everyone stayed indoors if possible, work halted, everyone had to wear a mask everywhere out of the home, and you had to quarantine in isolation if you contracted the virus. I am sure that I am missing a few other rules, but I highlight these for a reason.

From his prime-time national pulpit on *CNN*, "Fredo" hammered home these rules and more to his congregation of a television audience. Then, around March 31, 2020, "Fredo" contracted COVID-19. Here was an opportunity for "Fredo" to show his audience and the nation the discipline needed to practice what he preached: to follow quarantine protocols even after getting sick. What could be more interesting and compelling viewing for the time?

It wasn't great viewing:

> Some nights ["Fredo"] attempts to don the wartime mantle of his brother, New York Gov. Andrew [Cuomo]; other nights ["Fredo"] claims to be a broken man, relaying tales of shivering so hard he chipped a tooth, shedding 13 pounds in days, hallucinating conversations with his dead dad.

(Callahan, 2020). But, in between existential crises, "Fredo" maintained his daily drumbeat, leading the nation to believe he was dutifully following the rules he demanded of others. Except, he wasn't.

On Easter Sunday in 2020, and while still within the period he was to remain in quarantine, "Fredo" was out and about in the front yard of the East Hampton home he was constructing, alongside two women and three children (Concha, October 2020). A bicyclist named David Whelan was taking a break on a trail near the property when he spotted "Fredo":

> I just looked and said, 'Is that Chris Cuomo? Isn't he supposed to be quarantined? I said to him, 'Your brother is the coronavirus czar, and you're not even following his rules—unnecessary travel.

(Concha, April 2020). Whelan was correct. Not even a day before, "Fredo" had said on television that he just had a low-grade fever (Ibid.). In reaction to Whelan's temerity, an infected and mask-less "Fredo" approached him "like a boiling pot" (Creitz, 2020). "Fredo's" response left no doubt that "Fredo" was a full-blown Hypocrite:

> "Who the hell are you?! I can do what I want!" He just ranted, screaming, "I'll find out who you are!"

(Ibid.). The interaction left Whelan shaken enough for him to file a report with the East Hampton Police (Ibid.). "Fredo's" anger did not relent. He lost it again on his satellite radio show, lamenting the burdens of celebrity:

> I don't want some jackass, loser, fat-tire biker being able to pull over and get in my space and talk bullsh*t to me, I don't want to hear it.

(Concha, April 2020). Poor, poor "Fredo." Having to actually follow rules like a commoner and then be questioned by loser nobodies when he doesn't.

The Easter incident notwithstanding, "Fredo" thereafter staged a grand emergence from his quarantine in his basement for his adoring fans (Raymond, 2020). The farce included a walk up a flight of basement steps filmed by one of his children as he hugged his wife and younger children, who seemed less than amused (Ibid.).

I wonder why.

The cherry on top of this sundae of hypocrisy would come months later when "Fredo" called out President Trump for re-shooting his own re-emergence from COVID quarantine in October of 2020 (Tapp, 2020). "Fredo" called the admittedly staged moment "a bunch of bullsh*t" (Ibid.).

He would know.

REV. AL AVOIDS JUSTICE AFTER RAILROADING AN INNOCENT MAN

In 1987, Rev. Al was a chief defender of a Black teenager named Tawana Brawley. Brawley was found smeared with feces and scrawled with racial epithets, claiming she had been abducted and raped by a white gang (Chicago Tribune, 1998). Her allegations brought the bubbling pot of racial tension that was (The People's Republic of) New York to a boil, attracting national attention.

But Rev. Al, like he always does, cranked up the heat on the pot to eleven, causing it to overflow and scald innocents.

Rev. Al pointed a loud and accusatory finger at Steven Pagones, a prosecutor in Dutchess County, New York, as the culprit. All over the airwaves, Rev. Al recklessly tarred Pagones as a rapist and a kidnapper (Ibid.). But more importantly, Rev. Al proclaimed he had proof (Ibid.)

That proof never turned up, and Pagones was cleared when a grand jury returned with no charges (Ibid.). The evidence seemed to point to a hoax made up by Brawley, who wanted to avoid getting in trouble for staying out late (New York Times, 1998).

Justice may have prevailed, but Pagones and his family paid a heavy price. Pagones's career as a prosecutor was over, he and his family received constant death threats, and his marriage eventually broke up under the resulting stress and strain inflicted by Rev. Al and his minions (Klein, 2011). All Pagones had left was an opportunity to gain a measure of accountability. So, Pagones sued Brawley, Sharpton, and Rev. Al's inner circle for defamation (Goldman, 1998).

The case was long and tumultuous. Aside from the fierce exchange of insults between opposing counsel (Ibid.), one of the more interesting occurrences was how Rev. Al changed his tune. To the astonishment of all, Rev. Al stated that he never spoke directly to Tawana Brawley at any time while he insisted that he had proof of Pagones's guilt (Chicago Tribune). Sharpton went so far as to *claim he was the victim*, having been "duped" *by* Brawley. Rev. Al explained, "It would have been the height of ignorance to go to Tawana and say, 'Are your mother and father lying?'"

Um… yeah. That's actually what you should have done. It's called due diligence.

Ultimately, a jury saw through Rev. Al's claims of ignorance and victimhood, ordering Sharpton to pay sixty-five thousand dollars in damages for defaming Pagones with reckless disregard. Pagones doggedly pursued his money and eventually caught up to Rev. Al in 2001 (Wells, 2001).

But to this day, the Hypocrite remains unrepentant, having never apologized to Pagones for destroying his life.

CHAPTER 10

TRIGGER WARNING: BUFFOONICUS EXTREMIS

Life requires us to develop stress management skills. Every day, some combination of family, friends, colleagues, or strangers tests those skills. Most days, reasonable people respond by biting their tongue with their overbearing boss, sitting through the rubbernecking or changing the subject at the dinner table. But no one is perfect all the time. We all have those days where we snap, lean on our horn, and throw up some hand gestures, or instigate a screaming match that puts everyone off their appetite. When that happens, we atone appropriately and live with the consequences.

Now imagine if the script was flipped and remaining in a constant state of outrage was your default temperament with only occasional periods of lucidity. Imagine never apologizing for an outburst or an extreme statement. More importantly, imagine how others would act toward you if you were in a perpetual freak-out. They'd probably think you are…

THE LUNATIC

When we meet the Lunatic, she/he already possesses a delicate, albeit skewed, mental state. This is someone who has already breezed past the Hot Messes of the world in terms of Buffoonish Nature (BUN). Often, she/he already actively engages in politics on a regular basis either through activism or as an active observer. She/he is the product of confirmation bias, seeking out favorable partisan media that reassures the Lunatic she/he is on the right side of history, even though she/he is missing half of the story. Over time, wave after wave of tribalist influence leaves the Lunatic firmly entrenched within an extreme political perspective, and every social media "battle" that challenged his/her tribal views have made the Lunatic's skin paper-thin.

The typical freak-out has the same two-step process: the trigger and the emotional hijack. A trigger is:

> *something somebody says that you find offensive, judgmental, shaming or anxiety-producing; a behavior that hits a 'bruised bone' of yours; an overwhelming fear that you have been trying to suppress; a person, place, or thing that brings up a feeling of shame or fear—really anything that your deep brain deems as a threat.*

(Daughterty, 2020). Just think of any protest from the left from 2016 to the present, and you can probably conjure in your mind what a Lunatic freak-out can look like.

Next comes the emotional hijack, which throws one's emotional balance totally out of whack:

> *Everything... validates the trigger and you react as if it is the only truth. You may scream, cry, shut down, or worse. Further, you may feel overcome with a racing heart, a shot of adrenalin, a punch in the gut, or hot with rage or shame; discerning appropriate action from this state is virtually impossible. You may say or do something you regret later.*

(Ibid.). A Lunatic's emotional hijack may also include violence, like property destruction or even intentional infliction of physical and/or emotional harm. Just ask anyone currently living in Portland after the 2020 riots (Storyful Viral, 2021).

What truly separates the Lunatic from someone simply having a bad day is the difference in coping with a freak-out. While an average, reasonable person would recognize that a freak-out is your body's internal alarm blaring, the Lunatic seemingly believes their perpetual freak-out *is* the appropriate response. Instead of maintaining an open mind and honestly trying to discern a more appropriate response to the triggering impetus, the Lunatic maintains his/her death grip on those deeply ingrained tribal beliefs (which are often vulgar) while remaining righteous in his/her indignation and are, thus, prone to repeat the same inappropriate reactionary cycle, with vigor. It is no wonder that Lunatics occupy the higher reaches of the Sharpton Buffoonery MatrixTM; the emotions fueling the Lunatic's freak-out is like jet fuel propelling them up above the Sharpton-esque threshold in terms of BAM.

WHEN GETTING "POTTERIZED" HAD NOTHING TO DO WITH HOGWARTS

While many lionize the founders of our nation, let's not lose sight of the fact that America went through its share of growing pains before becoming the comparatively refined nation that we know today. Early Americans were indeed "rougher, simpler, more violent, more enterprising, [and] less refined" than their European counterparts (Williamson, 1972). Even the gentlemen of the day sometimes settled disputes with duels, especially because it was still legal in New Jersey. (Miranda, 2016). But enough quoting musicals.

By all accounts, Robert Potter was a brilliant and charismatic early American politician from North Carolina (Wheeler, 1851), but "his turbulent temper embroiled him in many difficulties" that would define his legacy (Ibid.). Potter "was a man of no ordinary powers of intellect," possessing both the gift of eloquence and the curse of a "fierce and ferocious temper" (Ibid.). He resigned from the Navy and started a law practice on his way to one of the craziest political careers in recorded American history (Ibid.).

In 1824, Potter ran for representative to the North Carolina House of Commons from the borough of Halifax in opposition to a man named Jesse Bynum (Ibid.). Those who knew Bynum and Potter say that both "possessed brilliant intellects, but because of violent tempers, they became involved in many difficulties that have brought reproach and almost ignominy upon their names" (Allen, 1918). They also say they carried on such a bitter personal rivalry all because Bynum had refused to introduce Potter to a young lady (Ibid.).

Here is where all that romanticizing about early America becomes relevant. Apparently, elections in Halifax provided "abundant opportunity for the exercise of electioneering—the kind most in vogue being drinking and fighting. Pistols and dirks were commonly used, and everybody looked for bloody accounts from a Halifax election" (Fayetteville Semi-Weekly Observer, 1859). As someone who has volunteered for several campaigns, I am glad this American tradition went by the wayside!

Potter lost, but like Stacey Abrams (Baily, 2020) on steroids, he freaked out, accusing Bynum of fraud and even challenging Bynum to a duel:

> *SIR: I forebore to chastise your insolence at the polls yesterday because I was unwilling to invoke my brave and devoted friends in the consequences of a quarrel with you. I understand you have renewed your vaporing today; indeed you appear to have a wonderful itching to riot in the van of mobs. This is to invite you to the field of combat. I cannot say that of honor, your presence would deprive any spot of that character. You can choose your own weapon and distance. My friend, Mr. Burges, will make the necessary arrangements with any person you may think proper for that purpose.*

(Fischer, 1976). Bynum refused to fight "on the grounds that Potter was not a gentleman," which fueled Potter's freak-out further (Wallace, 2021). He called Bynum "a poltroon and a coward" (Fischer, 1976).

As a side note, don't you wish we still spoke with such flourish? It's so much better than calling someone a "bitch" all the time.

The two men rematched in 1825. This election was even more of a disaster. On election day, Potter and his supporters got into a street fight with Bynum's crew, causing the entire election to be canceled in what came to be known as "hell in Halifax" (Allen, 1918). Sounds like something Vince McMahon promoted. One man died, and several were injured, including Potter, who had been stabbed with a sword, and Bynum, whose head was cracked (Ibid.). Both were arrested (Ibid.). The third time ended up being the charm for Potter, as he defeated Bynum in 1826, ending their trilogy.

Potter would lose re-election and moved from Halifax to Granville and won that seat in 1828 (Ibid.). After gaining some popularity in Granville, Potter would win election to Congress in 1830 but could not serve through his second term because he was sentenced to jail for one doozy of a crime (Ibid.).

Prior to running for Congress, Potter had taken a lovely bride from a "prominent family" named Isabella Taylor (Wallace, 2021). Mrs. Potter had two cousins who would be frequent visitors to her home; one was a Methodist minister in his mid-fifties, and the other was a seventeen-year-old boy (Fischer, 1976). Potter believed their frequent visits were not as innocent as they all would have him believe, if you catch my meaning (Ibid.).

If you haven't, you will soon.

On August 28, 1831, the elder cousin paid yet another visit, but this time, he was met by Potter, who proceeded to:

> [Lay] the charge of adultery on [him] and after a few angry words, pounced on him like a wild beast, beating him senseless. He then whipped out his keen, sharp blade and castrated the man, "potterized" him. Putting him to bed he told him if he would keep quiet his disgrace would not get out. "I have been very merciful and kind to you," Potter vouchsafed. "I have spared your life."

(Ibid.). Potter then traveled down the road a few miles and did the same thing to his wife's younger cousin. He "sprang upon him like a tiger, treating him as he had [the minister]" by tying him up and relieving him of his two best friends (Ibid.).

Yep, definitely a Lunatic freak-out.

Potter pled guilty to mayhem on the younger man, was imprisoned for six months, and was fined one thousand dollars (Wallace, 2021). His indictment for attacking the minister was deferred to see if Potter would face a murder charge. Mercifully (or not, depending on how you would perceive life after such violence), Potter's elder victim lived. In March of 1832, Potter pled guilty to assault with a deadly weapon and served two years in prison (Ibid.).

Somehow, Potter's criminal acts didn't end his political career. While in jail, Potter wrote a lengthy address to his constituency where he explained his justification for loping off his wife's cousin's dangling bits and claimed, as he did when he lost to Bynum a decade prior, that his prosecution and conviction was a political conspiracy (Ibid.). That particular freak-out landed Potter another indictment for libeling a judge (Ibid.).

Strangely, even after his history of brawling, paranoid freak-outs, maiming, and multiple terms in jail, the electorate in Granville County sent Potter back to the state legislature in 1834 (Allen, 1918). Again, Potter could not complete his term, as "highly injurious" reports emerged concerning a fight after a card game, during which he drew a pistol and a knife. Potter was expelled for actions "derogatory to the dignity" of the state legislature (Journal of the House of Commons, 1834).

So, just to recap, cutting off two guys' balls is not disqualifying for office, but fighting over cards gets you the boot. Wow.

In the end, "an unbridled will, a despotic temper and fierce revenge were the unguarded points by which he fell" (Wheeler, 1851). Potter "fled" to Texas to avoid further public ridicule (Allen, 1918) but rose to prominence yet again as the "founder" of the Texas Navy during the War of Texas Independence (Texas State Library & Archives Commission, 2021).

But alas, I must report that this Lunatic found a tragic end. After moving to Caddo Lake in Louisiana:

> [Potter] led a life of gross immorality, and, after forbearance had ceased to be a virtue, he was warned by his indignant neighbors to leave the community. He did not, however, obey the warning. Shortly afterwards a number of men come to his house by night, took him

> outside, and told him he richly deserved death; but they would give him a chance for his life. They then gave him a start of one hundred yards and told him that his life would be the forfeit if any of his pursuers should get in shooting distance of him. Potter immediately ran for the lake and plunged in to escape death by diving. His pursuers cane to the edge of the lake, and, as he came to the surface for breath, fired upon him and he sank to a watery grave,

(Allen, 1918). Thus, Robert Potter, an extreme Buffoonish Lunatic who had the capacity to use his words but woke up most days choosing violence, died "in disgrace and ignominy" (Ibid.).

Notice how I did not highlight any of Potter's political accomplishments. That's mainly because he had none.

AUNTIE MAXINE'S TROUBLED WATERS

All evidence to the contrary, Congress actually has rules for when members become outrageously out of order. The First Congress established the office of the Sergeant at Arms, who is tasked with maintaining decorum in the House Chamber (US House of Representatives, 2017). The House stipulated that "a proper symbol of office shall be provided for the Sergeant at Arms, of such form and device as the Speaker shall direct" (Ibid.). They settled on a mace, a bundle of thirteen rods adorned with a globe and a bald eagle, as the symbol of order and decorum (Ibid.). The Sergeant at Arms may use the mace upon the order of the Speaker whenever "an individual Member became turbulent and seemed beyond the Speaker's control" by having lifted the mace from its pedestal and "'presented' it before the offending person" (Ibid.). If the member ignores the presentation, she/he can be arrested, pursuant to House rules (US House of Representatives, 2021).

The last member of Congress who came the closest to seeing the Mace is one of Congress's loudest and most violent talkers: Rep. Maxine Waters (D-CA).

"Auntie Maxine," as she is known by partisan supporters, fits the profile of a Lunatic well; from her skewed, partisan views to her multiple triggers and the emotional hijack that quickly follows. One of her triggers is any perceived slight toward women. In July of 1994, Waters stood on the House floor uncontrollably denouncing Rep. Peter King (D-NY) over his alleged "badgering" of Hillary Clinton's chief of staff, Margaret Williams, whom King thought was lying during the House Banking Committee's hearings on the Whitewater affair (Manegold, 1994).

When Waters jumped in during the hearing, King said, "Why don't you just sit there?" (Ibid.). "You are out of order," Waters shot back (Ibid.). Not one to back down, King persisted, exclaiming that Waters is "always out of order" (Ibid.), to which, Waters said, "You are out of order. Shut up" (Ibid.).

Not one to be outdone, Waters persisted in her outrage on the House floor, declaring, "Men and women, the day is over when men can badger and intimidate women!" (Ibid.). As the decibel level and the hostility grew, Rep. Carrie Meek (D-FL), who was presiding over the House, raised her own voice in response, repeatedly rapping her gavel as she repeatedly told Waters, "You must suspend! You must suspend, gentlewoman!" (Ibid.). Eventually, Meek ruled that Waters "was out of order. The chair was about to direct the sergeant-at-arms to remove—to present the mace" (Ibid.). Ultimately, Speaker Thomas Foley (D-WA) slapped Waters on the wrist by keeping her off the House floor for the rest of the day (Ibid.).

Perhaps Waters's hottest trigger has been anything related to President Trump. As part of her multi-year crusade against all things Trump, Waters rallied supporters toward unreasonable, and possibly illegal, harassment of anyone pro-Trump:

> *If you see anybody from that cabinet in a restaurant, in a department store, at a gasoline station, you get out and you create a crowd. And you push back on them. And you tell them they're not welcome anymore, anywhere.*

(Ehrlich, 2018). After her comments, many members of the Trump administration faced targeted harassment, including White House spokesperson Sarah Sanders, Homeland Security Secretary Kirstjen Nielsen, and Labor Secretary Elaine Chao (Perkins, 2021). Someone even made "Wanted" posters targeting White House Senior Advisor Stephen Miller (Ibid.). Of course, Waters denied any causal connection between her words and anyone else's actions.

Waters's incendiary comments stand in stark contrast to her accusations against President Trump for his alleged incitement of Capitol protestors on the so-called Capitol "insurrection" on January 6, 2021 (Jacobs, 2021). Even in the face of video evidence, Waters remained indignant:

> Nothing any Democrat that I know of have ever said or acted in the way the president of the United States has acted.

(Ibid.). Keep telling yourself that, Auntie Maxine. The evidence speaks otherwise.

It's one thing to be an honest advocate for someone or a group of people. It's another to hate on other similarly situated people on your way to the top. The latter is a known poisonous tactic that Rev. Al tried to pass off as advocacy.

As we pointed out earlier, Rev. Al has never been above using "hate" as a means of communication. So, it shouldn't be surprising that Rev. Al has a history of engaging in dirty identity politics. While claiming to advocate for equal rights, Rev. Al has used ethnic innuendo and slurs to describe swaths of people during various speeches and sermons, including:

- "We're the Black chicken fryers of the universe. We gonna go buy some Colonel Sanders chicken. Then the Chinamen come in and throw some hot grease in the tub and dip it down and you stand by and buy that?" (Powe, 2014).
- "Koreans sell us watermelons. We been eating watermelon all our lives. They gonna come cut it up, put it in a bucket with a rubber band around it, and we gonna buy it like it's something we didn't know it was" (Ibid.).
- "White folks was in the cave when we had built empires. We taught philosophy and astrology and mathematics before Socrates and them Greek homos ever got around to it." (Benson, 2012).
- "David Dinkins, you want to be the only n***** on television, the only n***** in the newspaper, the only n***** that can talk. 'Don't cover them, don't talk to them,' 'cause you got the 'only n*****' problem. 'Cause you know if a Black man stood up next to you, they would see you for the whore that you really are" (Ibid.).
- "You ain't nothing! You a punk f****t!" (Joyella, 2010).

A particularly low moment came during a speech at Keene College in New Jersey, where Sharpton advocated killing white people. "I don't believe in marching. I believe in offing the pigs" (Dowling, 2016).

He reserved his most hateful diatribes for the Jewish population, which merits its own examination in our next chapter.

CHAPTER 11

THE WRETCHED REFUSE: BUFFOONICUS DETESTICUS

I have my share of personal stories concerning some particularly loathsome politicos. Like the time Republican party leaders from Queens and the Bronx thought it would be cool to pick up a padded envelope from the back of a limousine outside Sparks Steak House in exchange for their endorsement of a would-be mayor of New York City (Babcock and Calder, 2013). That turned out to be an FBI sting, and many people I knew went to jail (Ibid.).

Or like the story of a most-annoying gadfly named Joseph Hayon, who ran for Congress on a family values platform and was later convicted of possessing child pornography (Carrega, 2015). Ew.

But my absolute all-time favorite story from my time in politics involves a former Democratic assemblyman named William Boyland, who was convicted of corruption charges

(Casey, 2015) for soliciting bribes less than two weeks after he was acquitted of similar, but unrelated, charges to pay his lawyers who got him off the hook (Pillifant and Paybarah, 2014).

Yes, this actually happened, and it was all on tape.

These are but a mere sampling of the most loathsome and miserable type of Buffoons to come. Nothing is funny about these detestable cretins who possess no redeeming qualities. I call them…

THE RADIOACTIVE

This Buffoon is more defined by the ultimate outcome of their political misadventures than they are by the sum of them. When you carry the ones and arrive at the sum of the Radioactive's actions, we see that she/he caused such irreparable harm to their reputation, legacy, and/or credibility, that simply invoking their name recalls the awfulness of their loathsome activity. In extreme cases, even a distant connection to a Radioactive politico can spread the toxicity to others (Urban Dictionary, 2015).

The available paths during a political career are so wide ranging and varied that it is nearly impossible to define which carved-out routes will *always* result in political radioactivity. But we can make some general statements about certain character flaws that the Radioactive tends to possess. Pick a cautionary tale in politics, and you can identify some combination of these flaws. The arrogance of a Rod Blagojevich (Madhani, 2016), the self-destructive impulses of an

Anthony Weiner (aka "Carlos Danger"), the narcissism of John Edwards, (Dowd, 2008), or the sheer ignorance of a Rob Ford (Gee, 2013). The possibilities are literally endless.

The Radioactive is, in many respects, a close kin to the Egotist (*Buffoonicus ambitious*), so much so that the two are comparable to fraternal twins. One difference between these classifications is found by focusing on how loathsome the Buffoon and/or their action was, and, most importantly, how posterity weighs the acts against the balance of the Buffoon's public career. But perhaps the most significant difference between the two is that the Radioactive is capable of acts of Buffoonery with such disastrously high BAM that she/he can even impact the BUN of others situated within its fallout—even those who had not been considered Buffoons at all.

To further illustrate the point, let's briefly compare the fall of two high-profile politicians. First, consider Vito Fossella (R-NY), a bright politician who resigned from Congress in disgrace after a DUI led to the exposure of his double life, complete with separate families in different places (Barron, 2008). But after years on the periphery of politics, Fossella returned to elective office in 2021, winning election to the local office of borough president in Staten Island (Mathis-Lilley, 2021).

Now compare Fossella's tale to that of Senator Gary Hart (D-CO), a presidential front-runner who denied an extramarital affair by infamously challenging reporters to follow him around, only to be caught engaging in "monkey business" on a yacht of the same name (Gordon, 2021). Hart did not make it back into elective office but did put out a trial balloon at another presidential run, which did not go over well.

How can we explain that? Let's analyze Fossella and Hart with our Sharpton Buffoonery MatrixTM. Up to the point of their respective scandals breaking, both possessed relatively small BUNs, and both of their respective BAMs registered as Sharpton-esque. Fossella and Hart's respective acts concerned the relatively loathsome act of infidelity, and both remained active on the periphery of politics. Yet to date, society looked kindly on Fossella's successful comeback but looked poorly on Hart's float of another national run. This example leaves us with the hypothesis that the intensity of a Buffoon's radioactivity depends largely on the whims of public opinion. Anything beyond this superficial analysis requires deeper research into both case studies.

THE "KING OF THE COMSTOCK" WAS THE WORST SENATOR IN AMERICAN HISTORY

I know, that's a bold claim to make. But hear me out.

It has been said that the so-called "Gilded Age" of the late-nineteenth century in America was defined by the rapid expansion of American industrialization, which generated great wealth that "camouflaged massive poverty, moral decay, and corruption in politics and commerce" (Makley, 2006). This was the era of opulence, a "gold veneer" that covers an era of grift and greed (McLaughlin, 2018). Perhaps no one epitomized the darker side of this time in American history more than William Sharon.

To most, Sharon was an archetypal villain: the greedy, unscrupulous banker who used money and power for purely personal gain. At least one historian claims, "It is probably impossible to find a really kind word that was ever said about Sharon and preserved in print" (Makley, 2006).

Before running for office, Sharon "acquired enormous wealth while disguising the devious schemes required to gain it" (Ibid.). After bankrupting himself though high-risk stock speculation, Sharon become the Nevada agent for the Bank of California (McLaughlin, 2018). Through the bank, Sharon used financial leverage to gain control of the best mines working Nevada's Comstock Lode, the first major discovery of silver in the United States. Sharon and his associates would make low-interest loans to optimistic mining operations working the lode and would foreclose on those whose plans were a bit too optimistic (Ibid.). This resulted in Sharon controlling more than a dozen profitable mines (Makley, 2006). Sharon would then use his position to establish a railroad to monopolize transportation of the mined ore while "sticking Nevadans with years of tax debt to pay for it" (Keraghosian, 2021). Throw in the fact that Sharon was "[a] master at insider trading and business fraud" who used secret information from his network of mining foremen and superintendents to "capitaliz[e] on the rigged game of stock speculation," and it all added up to big money (McLaughlin, 2018). Sharon eventually became the head of the Bank of California and became infamously known as the "King of the Comstock."

Like many unscrupulous wealthy types, Sharon would turn to politics as a means to maintain his power and position, deciding to run for US Senate in Nevada, despite residing in San Francisco (Ibid.). But Sharon "was short, weighed 135 pounds, dressed like a minister in black broadcloth and rarely smiled." (Ibid.). Not exactly putting out "man of the people" vibes.

True to his business practices, Sharon played dirty on the campaign trail:

> *In his campaign he denigrated and made anti-Semitic remarks about his opponent, engineer Adolph Sutro, namesake of the legendary Comstock tunnel. He energized his white miner constituents with anti-Chinese rhetoric, a popular sentiment in the West at the time. Sharon even purchased the Gold Hill News whose new publisher, Alfred Doten... guaranteed editorial support for his candidacy.*

(Ibid.). Sharon eventually bought his way into the US Senate in 1875. To say that his tenure was a farce is an understatement.

> *Sharon's record in the United States Senate is one of the worst in the history of that legislative body. His record of inaction is unbelievable. He was seated at only five sessions and was recorded on less than 1 percent of all roll calls. He never introduced a bill and if he spoke on one it is not recorded. More important to Nevadans, he was absent from Washington during the important discussions on the silver question. His absences from Washington were exceeded only by those from the state he was supposed to present; his only visits to Nevada*

during his incumbency in the Senate came while passing though the state on his way to or from the east.

(Elliott and Rowley, 1987). "Senator" Sharon's political career was not a total waste of time. While in DC, he did manage to pick up some lovely real estate in what is now Dupont Circle and flip it for a huge profit (Lilley, 2021).

Sharon had one vice more that makes him the total package of scum and villainy. While running banks and mines and becoming a master of his universe, Sharon had a side hustle: sex.

Sharon began the [1860s] seeing Belle Warner, a local courtesan, on a regular basis. He helped her set up her own business, managing a string of young women on his behalf. He paid her a monthly retainer and regularly escorted Belle's employees to the Glenbrook Hotel... where he signed in as "Mr. Sharon and lady." It was a tidy little business in a small town with 49 saloons and an established prostitution district.

Nobody cared as long as there was no commotion.

(Ibid.). Sharon's libido would eventually lead to his final disgrace. Some twenty years after his aforementioned dalliances, a "[r]ich, old, and easily dazzled" (Ibid.) Sharon would fall prey to a young woman named Sarah Althea Hill, a young lady who would "cost him almost everything—his health, his prominence, his California residence, and the respect of his family" (Ibid.).

The details of the Sharon-Hill relationship are a book in and of itself. But here's the CliffsNotes version: The two held themselves out as a couple for many years until Sharon evicted Hill from their shared abode and proceeded to start seeing "no fewer than eight other women" (Ibid.). Obviously pissed, Hill would claim that Sharon married her in secret and had Sharon arrested for adultery (Ibid.). The two then became embroiled in a five-year matrimonial proceeding that "became one of the era's most high-profile and ill-fated court cases" and "[b]y the time the dust settled, Sharon had died, Sarah had gone insane, court bailiffs had been beaten up, a former chief justice of the state supreme court was jailed and then shot by a US Marshal, and a United States Supreme Court Justice was attacked" (Ibid.).

Ruthlessness. Selfishness. Amorality. Insanity. That's definitely a recipe for Radioactivity.

Ambrose Bierce, a short story writer and journalist, would give Sharon a rather pointed sendoff later in life suitable for a Radioactive Buffoon:

> *Sharon, some years, perchance, remain of life-*
> *Of vice and greed, vulgarity and strife;*
> *And then-God speed the day if such His will-*
> *you'll lie among the dead you helped to kill,*
> *And be in good society at last,*
> *Your purse unsilvered and your face unbrassed.*

(Bierce, 2019). So, there you go. If you can find a worse politician, then I'd be glad to hear you out.

UPHOLDING NEW YORK'S PLACE AS THE CAPITAL OF CORRUPTION

Here's some trivia for you: Did you know that the last governor of "The People's Republic of" New York to be voted out of office in an election was Mario Cuomo in 1994 when a relatively unknown state senator named George Pataki defeated him (Gladwell, 1994)? Since then:

- Pataki chose not to run for a fourth term;
- that "fucking steamroller" Eliot Spitzer resigned as "Client No. 9"; and
- Spitzer's successor, David Paterson, withdrew from his campaign amid news that his administration improperly intervened in a domestic violence case against one of his closest aides (Hakim and Peters, 2010).

But even in "The People's Republic of" New York, hope springs eternal, just as it did when Andrew Cuomo was first elected in 2010. Immediately, Cuomo stated his intention to turn the tide of corruption in Albany. "The people want a government of competence and performance and integrity," he correctly declared (Miranda, 2015).

It certainly would have been a welcome change. Good government groups and everyday citizens had cause for optimism when Cuomo created a Commission to Investigate Public Corruption under the state's Moreland Act with the goal to "probe systemic corruption and the appearance of such corruption in state government, political campaigns and elections in New York State" (State of New York, December 2021). The Commission was to be, in the Governor's own words, "totally independent" of political interference:

> Anything they want to look at, they can look at—me, the lieutenant governor, the attorney general, the comptroller, any senator, any assemblyman

(Craig, et. Al., 2014). Spoiler: It wasn't. Cuomo blatantly interfered with the commission's work, even hamstringing investigators who had the temerity to focus on groups with ties to Cuomo and his campaigns (Ibid.). And my, did Cuomo change his tune after he shut down the commission:

> It's not a legal question. The Moreland Commission was my commission," Mr. Cuomo explained. "It's my commission. My subpoena power, my Moreland Commission. I can appoint it, I can disband it. I appoint you, I can un-appoint you tomorrow. So, interference? It's my commission. I can't 'interfere' with it, because it is mine. It is controlled by me.

(Crain's New York, 2014). So much for transparency and independence.

Yet Cuomo won a third term in 2018, during which he would position himself as a foil to President Donald Trump, especially during the COVID-19 pandemic in 2020. Many found some reassurance in the routine that Gov. Cuomo's daily televised briefings developed during a very uncertain spring (Milligan, 2020), while others fell for Andrew's charming appearances on the aforementioned "Cuomo Brothers Comedy Hour" on *CNN* (Concha, 2020) or on late-night television talking relationships with Jimmy Fallon (Niemietz, 2020).

It was the summer of the "Cuomosexual" (Carras, 2020).

While Cuomo reveled in new-found popularity with his weird "flatten the curve" poster (Cole, 2020) and his multi-million-dollar book deal (Goodman, et. Al., 2021), New York was at the epicenter of the pandemic with over thirty thousand casualties before the fall of 2020.

Or so we thought. The actual numbers were much, much worse.

It turned out that "America's Governor" was hiding the state's true death toll. In March of 2020, Cuomo's Department of Health issued an "Advisory" stating that no resident shall be denied re-admission or admission to the health facilities, like nursing homes, "solely based on a confirmed or suspected diagnosis of COVID-19" (Berdzik, et. Al., 2020). Effectively, Cuomo forced the most vulnerable population of New Yorkers to be heavily exposed to a deadly virus.

Cuomo compounded his errors by lying about the true extent of the death toll his order caused. The state's attorney general issued a report in January of 2021 claiming that nursing home resident deaths appear to be undercounted by DOH by approximately 50 percent (State of New York, January 2021). But even "killing grandma" was not enough to turn Cuomo Radioactive (McManus, 2020). Though damaged by the nursing home scandal, Cuomo persevered to the dismay of many (McKinley, 2021).

It took a boatload of claims of sexual harassment uncovered in a second report from the state attorney general to do that (State of New York, August 2021). One after another, women started coming forward claiming that Gov. Cuomo made inappropriate and unwanted advances of affection.

Equally as creepy was Cuomo's response to these multiple allegations. He started out by using the classic "I'm Italian" defense for his touchy-feely ways, complete with a video montage that skeeved out observers further (Dante, 2021). Then, circling the wagons, Cuomo called upon an inner circle comprises of state employees and outside associates to act as his crisis team. Among those picked to craft Gov. Cuomo's message were:

- Dani Lever, a former Cuomo staffer now working at Facebook who secretly advised his former boss to "shame" his accusers (Wayt, 2021);
- his brother, the aforementioned Hypocrite Chris "Fredo" Cuomo, who used his press contacts to dig up dirt on his brother's accusers (Baragona, 2021);

- Alphonso David, then-president of the gay rights group Human Rights Campaign, who provided a confidential file on former Cuomo aide Lindsey Boylan to a press aide, (Schwartz, 2021); and
- Tina Tchen, a former adviser to Michelle Obama and then-CEO of Time's Up, an organization whose aim is to "create a society free of gender-based discrimination in the workplace and beyond" (Time's Up, 2021), who along with Roberta Kaplan, a founder of Time's Up's Legal Fund, reviewed a draft of a disparaging op-ed letter targeting Boylan. (Kantor and Gold, 2021).

David, "Fredo," Tchen, and Kaplan were all relieved of their respective employment in the blast radius of Andrew Cuomo's scandals and subsequent resignation for which he will forever go down in infamy.

In 1991, Rev. Al defended Leonard Jeffries, a City College professor who said during a particularly hateful speech that "everyone knows rich Jews helped finance the slave trade" (Mandel, 2019), and that "Russian Jewry had a particular control over the movies, and their financial partners, the Mafia, put together a financial system of destruction of Black people" (Cohen, 1993).

Sharpton fanned the flames of Jeffries' anti-Semitism by spewing some of his own. "If the Jews want to get it on, tell them to pin their yarmulkes back and come over to my house," Sharpton declared (Mandel, 2019).

What happened next is a calamity of tragedy that set New York City ablaze in racial violence.

In the Crown Heights neighborhood of Brooklyn, a Jewish driver accidentally struck and killed a seven-year-old Black boy named Gavin Cato (Myrphy, 2021). The accident was the flashpoint of three days of anti-Semitic rioting where Jewish scholar Yankel Rosenbaum was stabbed to death. According to published reports, Rev. Al was front and center in the streets of Crown Heights leading marches that included chants of "No justice, no peace!" and "Kill the Jews!" (Ibid.).

Disgusting? Yes. But this is not a discussion of mob mentality, so let's not hold Rev. Al to the actions of others. What I will do is judge Rev. Al by his own words. Rev. Al was in rare form at young Gavin's funeral:

> *The world will tell us he was killed by an accident. Yes, it was a social accident. It's an accident for one group of people to be treated better than another group of people. It's an accident to impose the will of a minority on a majority. It's an accident to allow an apartheid ambulance service in the middle of Crown Heights. It's an accident to think we will just keep crying and not stand up and call for justice*

> *Talk about how Oppenheimer in South Africa sends diamonds straight to Tel Aviv and deals with the diamond merchants right here in Crown Heights. The issue is not anti-Semitism; the issue is apartheid. ... All we want to say is what Jesus said: If you offend one of these little ones, you got to pay for it. No compromise, no meetings, no kaffeeklatsch, no skinnin' and grinnin'.*

(Jewish Journal, 2011; Mendel, 2019). For the uninitiated, Rev. Al's reference to "diamond merchants" was a veiled shot at Jewish jewelers in New York City. After an investigation, the young Jewish driver at the heart of this tragedy, Yosef Lifsh, was not indicted on any criminal charges and left for Israel (Chicago Tribune, 1991).

Sharpton flew to Israel to serve Lifsh with a wrongful death civil suit. According to the *NY Daily News*, a woman at Ben Gurion Airport in Tel Aviv spotted Sharpton and shouted, "Go to hell!"

Sharpton yelled back, "I am in hell already" (Ibid.).

Years later, Sharpton's views on the Jewish people would pop up again. Rev. Al was invited to speak at the Religious Action Center's Consultation on Conscience, much to the anger of Jewish leaders (Kampeas, 2021). Sharpton paid a *mea culpa*, acknowledging that he could have "done more to heal rather than harm" in his past dealings (Ibid.).

You don't say.

Many Jewish leaders expressed their dismay and anger in reaction, calling the attempt to "wash away" the pain Rev. Al had caused "cruel" (Ibid.).

Clearly, some radioactive stains don't ever wash away.

SO... WHAT DID WE LEARN?

As I said when you got on this wacky ride, the goal was to create a work of satire, pointed by truth. So where does this exercise leave us? I have a few ideas to consider as we come to the close.

HISTORY DOESN'T REPEAT, BUT IT RHYMES
A theme that surprised me while researching is that the things we believe to be modern problems within society, have existed for decades, if not centuries, in American society.

Unlike what today's media has been trying to tell you, the concept of "fake news" is far from a new phenomenon. The antagonism between the media and partisans goes back even to our founding, just as advocates masquerading as journalists have. These issues remain mostly unsolved. The main difference between past generations and today is that we have more access to information than ever before at a speed never seen before. We both transmit and consume information faster.

Also, bad politicians have always existed who have goals to either keep their position of power or obtain a better one. Same with dumb politicians who say a whole lot yet say nothing at all, and politicians who stick their foot in their mouth, who lash out at political opponents in anger, who have philandered and been underhanded and have committed just about every kind of wrongdoing under the sun. We just hear more about them now.

Finally, we have developed an arrogance about ourselves in comparison to our predecessors. We like to think of ourselves as more enlightened than past generations. After all, no one engages in duels anymore, and certainly fewer of us are brawling outside of polling places. But if we are being honest, we have no moral high ground. More people are quicker to choose violence to make their political points than we as a society would care to admit. Just look at the "summer of love" in Seattle in 2020, or the one hundred days of burning in Portland. And yes, more politicians are more freely using vulgarities in public than when many of us were growing up. That shows, if anything, a return to the rough-and-tumble days of the politics of days past.

All in all, our examination of these case studies in Political Buffoonery has shown that when it comes to identifying what's wrong with American politics, not much has changed over time.

Isn't it funny how many of us lament how bad today's politics have turned look back on the past with such rose-colored glasses? Yet simultaneously, those same people believe that our generation is somehow superior to those backward times—times of clinging to guns and Bibles and such. Perhaps it is high time that we drop this arrogant veneer of superiority, recognize that nothing new is under the sun as it pertains to American political culture, and turn to the real question that we should be asking: What is it about today's American culture that has caused a seeming explosion in Political Buffoonery?

ENTITLEMENT CULTURE BREEDS BUFFOONS
When you think about every classification of Buffoonery covered regardless of time period, each Buffoonish act found roots in the Buffoon's sense of entitlement, some unearned sense of self-confidence, some belief in personal superiority, or some other kind of hubris or sense of personal privilege.

Seeing this, my humble suggestion for solving our Political Buffoonery problem is to address the generational problem of "entitlement culture." As professor Ramani Durvasula wrote in 2019:

> *Entitlement is at its core a toxic characteristic. It is the assumption that a person deserves special treatment, is exempt from the rules, and should not be held to the same standards (behavioral or otherwise) as others. Entitlement is generally synonymous with wealth and power and proliferates amongst those at the top of the hierarchy.*

How one develops this toxic characteristic is not exactly clear. In an article for the *Character and Context Blog* of the Society for Personality and Social Psychology from 2019, Emily Zitek tells us that while science does not fully understand the sources of entitlement, researchers have identified external factors that may contribute to its development, ranging from how your parents and other authority figures treated you and life events that made you feel special, to even messages from the media.

I believe we have developed a generation of entitled individuals. In 2014, *Reason* conducted an opinion poll about what phrases best describes today's millennials. Two-thirds of respondents said that "entitled" describes millennials at least somewhat well, and 70 percent said "selfish" worked too (Ekins, 2014). When broken down by partisan affiliation, 64 percent of Democrats believe millennials are "hard-working" with 52 percent of Republicans saying the term was not a good fit (Ibid.).

But here's what was most striking by the poll: Even the majority of millennials polled agreed that both "selfish" and "entitled" summed them up well (Ibid.). And why wouldn't they? Millennials are the generation of those who "demand or expect things too fast instead of being patient and respectful," which "only expose[s] their naiveness" (Jenkins, et. al., 2016). I agree with Zitek; I blame those ridiculous so-called "helicopter parents" who unreasonably coddled their precious little ones and bent to their every whim for this trend. You know the type; the ones who couldn't bear to let their ten-year-old "baby" out of their site.

Millennials are also the generation of participation trophies where merit was reduced to just showing up (Blake, 2014). The same poll tackles this topic in connection to this cultural perception of "entitlement" as well. A strong majority of Americans said that only winners in youth sports should get trophies. But interestingly enough, when you break down the results by income strata, those earning less than thirty-thousand dollars per year preferred participation trophies 55 to 42. (Ibid.). Just as a quick reminder, Democrats have a huge voter enrollment advantage among those earning less than fifteen thousand dollars per year, which also carries forward to those earning up to fifty thousand dollars per year (Fay, 2021). No wonder millennials flock to those accepting arms of Democrats and away from the rejection of Republicans who value, among other traits, merit and personal achievement (Wilson, 2021).

If you had any question why Democrats are perceived to be the party of entitlement, I hope these numbers put that issue to bed. Perhaps that is why, in my opinion, while neither party has a monopoly on Political Buffoonery, the majority of observed Buffoonish acts originate from the left side of the aisle—because that's where the entitled find their safe spaces.

That said, how do we push back against entitlement culture in general?

LET'S PUT CHARACTER AND CREDIBILITY FIRST

I see the struggle between merit and entitlement as central to the culture war in America. If achievement is not earned and if goals are met without struggle, then values never take hold, and the opportunity to develop personal character is lost.

G. Michael Hopf once wrote, "Hard times create strong men, strong men create good times, good times create weak men, and weak men create hard times." I tend to agree with that; as William Strauss and Neil Howe observed, history is defined by a "seasonal rhythm of growth, maturation, entropy, and rebirth."

The hard times of World Wars I and II created strong men and women who answered the call to defend our way of life. There is a reason we call them "The Greatest Generation." Those strong men and women created the good times for the generations that followed. Those of us who benefited from those good times rarely had to step up to meet any challenges anywhere near the magnitude that past generations did. While a teenager in the 1940s may have been shipped overseas to face certain death, today's twenty-somethings throw a fit when their internet connection drops momentarily in the middle of *Call of Duty*. Many believe we are living in the middle of that transition point to bad times brought on by weak people. If the proliferation of entitlement culture is any indicator (to speak nothing of the growing ideological divide in today's political discourse and the growing tensions around the world), those beliefs are accurate.

If you see the same cyclical nature of history, then it's time to step up. The struggles associated with today's entitlement culture can only be addressed by those who confront them head on—not in the streets or on a battlefield, but in your own private and public life.

It's time to get back to valuing character in our personal lives. Lead by example by being an honest and trustworthy person to show the stark contrast between meritocracy and entitlement. Be the role model that someone was to you so those who look up to you will want to be like you instead of the entitled personality on the screen. Don't settle for being seen as relevant; be relevant.

Publicly, we as voters need to consider a candidate's character as much as we consider accomplishments. Explore their upbringing and background. Did they struggle to succeed, or did success come easily? What did they learn from failure?

Finding character in others means effectively weighing credibility. Given the explosion of Political Buffoonery, we have done a collectively poor job at that, so here's a short refresher. Aristotle divided the means of persuasion into logos, pathos, and most importantly, ethos. Ethos is the messenger's gravitas—a combination of knowledge with moral authority and expressed good will (Umeogu, 2012). Some might even call it sincerity.

Whatever you call it, finding genuinely credible people to lead should be our goal. I get that it will be hard to discern a genuinely credible person in a world where ethos is more a portrayal of carefully crafted messages and polished imagery than a personal trait developed through struggle and merit. That's why it takes a person of character to tell the difference; only real recognizes real. So, start within, so the rest becomes clearer.

Oh, and one more thing.

LIMIT GOVERNMENT, LIMIT BUFFOONS

Invariably, our ability to detect bull from a candidate will fail us and some Buffoons will be elected to office. Therefore, we need a further backstop against those Buffoons who get by us. The best way to do just this is to limit the power a Political Buffoon can wield.

Now, I can give you the typical arguments of how limiting government would maximize opportunity, enterprise, and creativity (Reed, 2004). But I'm not. This argument for limited government in this context is simple: If government had less control over our everyday lives, we would not have to deal with these damn Buffoons as often as we do.

In a speech to The Heritage Foundation, public policy wonk Larry Reed once said the "silly side" of politics is "characterized by no-speak, doublespeak, and stupid-speak: the use of one's tongue, lips, and other speechmaking body parts to sway minds without ever educating them—and to deceive them, if necessary" (Ibid.). There is, as we know, a darker side as well. Politics differentiates itself from private undertakings in that "the politician's words are backed up by his ability to deploy legal force on their behalf" (Ibid.). An apocryphal quote traditionally attributed to George Washington warns us that:

> Government is not reason, it is not eloquence—it is force. Like fire it is a dangerous servant and a fearful master; never for a moment should it be left to irresponsible action.

(Volokh, 2010). Or, irresponsible Buffoons for that matter.

If nothing else, the COVID-19 pandemic and all the restrictions placed on our everyday lives provided us with a stark reminder of that very idea. The fire that is government becomes all the more fearful to individuals when brandished by a Buffoon. That is why the fire itself must also be tended to carefully.

And with that, I guess we're done...

WAIT! WHAT ABOUT TRUMP?

You didn't think I would write a book about Political Buffoonery and not devote some discussion to President Donald Trump, did you? So, let's ask the question most of you were probably thinking about when you got this book: Is Donald Trump a Buffoon?

The answer, of course, is yes. Because as discussed at the outset, we *all* are Buffoons. Each one of us is fallible. Each one of us is prone to embarrassing moments of Buffoonery. The question that remains concerns degree only.

But yes, a case can certainly be made that President Trump committed several Buffoonish acts and indeed has a significant Buffoonish nature. No one could dispute his penchant for puffery and over-exaggeration, or his desire to take credit for any and all successes. Who can forget his complaints over frivolous matters like the measurement of crowd size at an event?

For goodness sakes, his name is prominently displayed on every building, right? If all of this does not scream *Buffoonicus oblivious*—the Narcissist—I don't know what does.

That said, consider this possibility: Despite these personal foibles, is President Trump *just* a Buffoon, or does he also *play* the Buffoon?

There is something to be said about using perceived Buffoonery as a lever of power. No less than Niccolò Machiavelli in his *Discourses on Livy* wrote "that it is a very wise thing to simulate craziness at the right time." Even President Nixon contemplated in his memoir "the importance of being unpredictable when dealing with the Communists" during his tenure. Trump seemingly took a similar tact of "rational irrationality" (Matthews, 2017) in quieting the mounting threat of North Korea. He even told Vladimir Putin, "If you move against Ukraine while I'm president, I will hit Moscow" (Goodwin, 2022).

Social anthropologist Mark Leopold explored a similar idea and posited that a political leader, including despots, may take on the airs of a more Buffoonish nature to:

- lead opponents to underestimate the leader's ability and intelligence;
- provide deniability within the confines of alleged humor;
- appeal to core supporters as a way to take a perceived adversary down a notch or two in their estimation;
- serve to distract from more serious, perhaps frightening or incompetent, actions, also known as "deadcatting" (Milbank, 2017); and
- create ambiguity, confusion, and/or uncertainty about how to respond.

I am sure as you are reading this list that you can immediately think of some instance where some unorthodox Trump act could fall into this category.

Did President Trump use Buffoonery to lead opponents into underestimating him? Of course. Think of all the primary opponents that then-candidate Trump left in his wake. Think of Jeb (exclamation point!) Bush's dumbfounded face as he couldn't figure out why his own popularity waned while Trump's star rose with each low-brow insult he laid into him (Killough, 2016). In fact, when you think about it, who didn't underestimate President Trump at one time or another because of some outward appearance of Buffoonery? Almost too many examples come to mind that would illustrate the point.

In fact, *Slate*'s Yascha Mounk once noted a year into the Trump presidency:

> *We've underestimated Trump over and over and over again. And over and over and over again, we've all paid a heavy price. And yet, many of the same pundits and political scientists who confidently predicted that Trump would never be president are now confidently predicting that his presidency will soon be tanked by incompetence and unpopularity.*

Did President Trump use Buffoonery for plausible deniability? Definitely. In 2016, Trump "encouraged" Russia to hack Hillary Clinton in 2016 and later claimed it was a joke (Cohen, 2018). In 2018, Trump intimated that Democrats were "treasonous" for sitting through his State of the Union without clapping and later claimed it was a joke (Smith, 2018). In 2019, Trump told the press on the White House lawn that China should investigate Joe Biden and his family because "what happened in China is just as bad as what happened in Ukraine" (Borger, 2019), referring to Hunter Biden's involvement in a fund drawing investment from the Bank of China, and later claimed it was a joke (Baker and Sullivan, 2019). Trump "joked" like this several other times, which became an effective test balloon for a variety of iffy positions and potential political narratives (Singer, 2020).

Did President Trump use Buffoonery as a rallying cry for supporters to look negatively on an opponent? I think a better question is whether President Trump did anything *but* that. I need not go in depth into the phenomenon that is the Trump rally; I'll let John Baer remind you:

> *Donald Trump's rallies ... have a ritualistic ring of religion.*
>
> *The chants. The music. The amen-like affirmations. The same prayers: build the wall, drain the swamp and (yes, still) lock her up, or lock somebody up. The call-and-response to boo the media for dishonesty and "fake news."*
>
> *And, more recently, condemning the "witch hunt" by Democrats and the deep state and the litany of nicknamed enemies: Shifty Schiff, Nervous Nancy, Sleepy Joe, Mini Mike, Pocahontas, Crooked Hillary, et al.*

Yeah, you remember.

Did President Trump use Buffoonery as a distraction? One word: Twitter. It seemed like the more outrageous a Trump tweet was, the more his opponents in the media covered it. Trump could seemingly call upon this power at will, and the press seemed to become addicted to the coverage. Margaret Sullivan believed "journalists… tended to over-respond to every tweet, in some ways treating them as five-alarm fires when few of them deserve to be that" (Ingram, 2017).

Finally, did President Trump use Buffoonery to instill confusion or uncertainly in an adversary? His mere existence continues to cause chaos and confusion among Democrats to this day. Memories of past tactics used during his presidency have left today's Democrats chasing a boogeyman, even after removing him from office in the 2020 election. "Democrats are ignoring [the) real issues facing Americans today," said Rep. James Comer (R-KY) on the floor of the Congress (Jones, 2021). "Instead, Democrats want to talk about former President Trump, even though a Democrat has occupied the White House for nearly a year" (Ibid.).

Look no further than the Virginia gubernatorial race of 2021 for proof that Comer is right. Democratic nominee Terry McAuliffe ran a campaign against Donald Trump instead of his actual opponent and eventual governor Glenn Youngkin, which voters saw as a stretch at best (Moomaw, 2021). Virginia delegate Sam Rasoul (D-Roanoke) hit the nail squarely on the head when he said, "We spend entirely too much time talking about Donald Trump and not articulating not only our vision for the future but spending time genuinely connecting with people and with their needs" (Ibid.).

In this humble Buffoonologist's opinion, Trump, a flawed Buffoon though he may be, wielded Political Buffoonery like a freakin' Jedi master. Political Buffoonery became both President Trump's sword and his shield in the blood sport that is American politics.

OKAY. NOW, WE ARE DONE!

I hope this examination of Political Buffoonery is only the beginning of a wider journey that sees you become more politically aware and ever vigilant. Do not allow one of the many wonderous varieties of Buffoons we identified come along and screw things up for all of us.

No pressure.

ACKNOWLEDGMENTS

I have so many people to acknowledge for making this book happen. But here goes.

Of course, the list starts at home with my family. From a young age, my parents, Robert and Barbara Berardelli, were the living embodiment of love and support in every endeavor I pursued. Even the stupid ones. Mom and Dad helped me succeed, gave me space to learn from failure, and were my number-one fans. It's a guarantee that Mom has already started tearing up as she reads this. Please know how much I love you, even when I'm too busy to show it. Let's both laugh through the tears as we picture Dad and Grandpa up in Heaven bragging about this!

To my fantastic sister, partner in crime, museum nerd, and editor extraordinaire Linda Berardelli, who has put up with me on a daily basis for nearly forty years: Every day, I am in awe of the person you've become and how you doggedly persist, earning everything you deserve. Thank you for kicking me in the ass just enough for me to get out on this particular limb.

To my nephew and best friend, Marcos Antonio, it has been the greatest honor of my life watching you grow up into an amazing young man. Thank you for laughing at every dad joke, for every pizza exploration, for letting me tag along on Pokémon GO walks, and for every hug, every funny selfie, and every other moment ever. You're the best, Bubba!

To John Pennisi, thank you for bringing my crazy visions to life. I cannot say enough about how you brought my work into focus in a way no one else could have. Thank you for picking up the phone for a guy contacting you out of the blue after so many years.

To Evan Sayet, who has been an inspiration at the crossroads of politics and culture to many people, including me. I am humbled that you have lent your imprimatur to my work. But seriously, did you have to write so much better than me? I mean, really... Everyone must read the foreword and experience Evan's gift for witticism and eloquence.

A special thanks to the team at New Degree Press for putting all the pieces together. That especially means you, Lauren Sweeney, and you, Chuck Oexmann. But also, the copy editing team, the layout team, the cover design team; I can't say enough good things about them. Thank you all for your patience during the hours we spent together because you believed in the work and not just because my sister may have threatened you.

Now, to the good stuff: all the people responsible for getting this book published!

I have been blessed in life to have met so many people whom I consider family more so than most of my blood relations. To the "Forefathers of Buffoonology," Russell and Diana Gallo, Amanda Kohut, and Matthew Fairley, I could fill an entire book about what you each mean to me. I'm sure you all know this already. But just so it's memorialized in print for all time, everything I ever said and did in those years with you working in Brooklyn, in New York State, in Washington and/or all points in between, please know that it was, actually, all Russ's fault. Thank you for every radio show, every YR meeting, every late night working on a campaign (including the "black ops" we'll never admit to doing). Thank you for making every meeting where we were the youngest people in the room bearable and, especially, for every drunken night where flowers were eaten, hot tubs bubbled over, and the fun never ended.

To Craig Eaton, thank you for your mentorship, your unwavering support for just about every caper I cooked up, and, especially, for your endless patience for my own Buffoonery, which may or may not have included the occasional mislabeling of what day of the week went with whatever calendared event we had going on at the time.

To Mark Healey, thank you for taking a risk on a kid fresh out of law school and trusting me with your dream. You taught me how to chase my own.

To Lynn and Vince Casale, the most generous people in politics. In a game filled with gatekeeping vipers jockeying to become kings of their respective hills, you showed me that good people can still make it. I am constantly amazed that, despite the intensely active political lives you lead, you always made time for me both professionally and personally. Offering thanks feels so insufficient, but please know I am forever grateful to you both.

To Jack Buckby and Martina Markota, watching you both go through your own trials and tribulations while remaining so optimistic about life is a constant source of inspiration. Your support for this crazy project is unmatched. Thank you for also introducing me to your friends, David Solimano, Nicole Leavitt, and Douglas Nelson, who, without knowing me, supported my book just based on your recommendation. Thank you, David, Nicole, and Douglas. I look forward to getting to know you better and bringing you in on all the fun.

My time in politics would not have been nearly as fun without this "crew." While I am sad that time, distance, and circumstances have kept us apart more often than not lately, know that I will never forget the love and support from all of you:

- Vito Palmeri and Vito DiGiovanni/Vito DiGiovanni and Vito Palmeri: I couldn't decide whom to list first without offending the "other Vito." Thanks for the thousands of miles logged over the years, for all the items stolen from housekeeping (who takes a vacuum?), and for not letting me ever feel my age.
- Jonathan Lubecky: a friend who has always had my back. I marvel daily at your accomplishments, and I thank you for helping me achieve mine.
- Anne Gallo: Don't tell anyone, but you're my favorite Gallo.

- Mike Tracey: Thank you from being there from the start and for forever changing what a Kansas Jayhawks basketball jersey means to me for all time.
- Alicia and Zachery Sirk: always of the same mind as me when it comes to who are real leaders and who are fake Buffoons. Thank you for being examples of the former, and for always calling out the latter, even if it means offending the "cool kids."
- Michelle Gallo: Don't tell anyone, but you're my favorite Gallo.
- Jacob Bard: The Spy! Keep daring to dream big and never stop being the "Yak Attack" we all know and love. But on a seven, not a ten.
- Ken Rice: Why you let yourself get roped into our crazy political world, I'll never know. But thanks for always being the sane one.
- Kara Walker: always the kindest person in any room! Thank you so much for your insight and your friendship.
- Timothy Furey: As you sit on a beach somewhere basking in your brilliance with dreams of making all the money, please know how glad I am for knowing you. And send money.

To those who are part of my "CPAC family," people I met in Washington, DC, though the years who have supported me ever since:

- Steve Stockman: Talk about a ride. Thank you for so many lasting memories, including those I will never put pen to paper to explain!
- Brad Marston: one of the best men I know. Thank you for your sage political advice, your infectious passion, and

for lending me your concept for one legendary night in DC that you made happen.
- Rob Towner: a true gentleman. Thanks for reminding me some good people are still left in DC.
- Vivek Subramanyam: It's been a pleasure to see you grow into a promising young attorney. Thank you for supporting this book; please don't give it a bad review.
- Bradford Belk: I hope you know how much of an inspiration your "Less Government, More Fun" concept was for my book. Your unwavering support will never be forgotten.
- Jennifer Ann Massey: I'm glad our mutual friend connected us, but I have to admit, I was a little star struck! Seeing you become a political player in your own right has been awesome. I'm glad to be able to say, "I knew her when…"
- Jonathan Hanen: my favorite "wonk." Thank you for nerding out with me through the years on air and the laughs off air.

I only have so much room left! Word counts stink! So, forgive me if I didn't include a funny or poignant remark. Hopefully, you already know how I feel toward all of you.

Before politics got a hold of me, these wonderful people saw something in me (I couldn't tell you what) earlier in my life and, for some reason, they stuck around. For that, I am forever grateful:

- Zhenya Pinkusovich: forever my "boss." I'm not me without you.
- Christopher Trivino

- Paul Greco
- Roberto Mignone
- Teddy Dziuba

To my friends in local, state, and national politics who fight the good fight every day by showing everyone what leadership looks like:

- Mary Therese Reilly
- John Burnett
- William F.B. O'Reilly
- Robert Howe
- Garrett Murch (author of *Ezzy's Education,* which everyone should check out)

To my friends online who share my passion to endlessly converse about the politics of the day. Each and every time we talked online added a little extra something to my thoughts for this book:

- Sammy Hahn: who calls me his mentor for some reason, but who has taught me just as much as he claims that I taught him.
- David Jaroslav
- Ryan Girdusky
- Jenny Kefauver
- Kristie Tertel: an unstoppable force of nature who slays it daily while still making time to chat with little ol' me.
- Timothy Shea
- Amie Mocere
- Nancy Joseph
- Sara Graf

- Hillary Seeger
- Deanna Duncan
- Jeff Reynolds

And a special thanks to those who disagree with me on… well, just about any political issue, but supported me nonetheless. Thomas Jefferson once wrote that he "never considered a difference of opinion in politics, in religion, in philosophy, as cause for withdrawing from a friend." Thank you for embodying that spirit; you are maddeningly appreciated!

- Michael Treybich
- Igor Kuperman
- Linda Sarsour

Luckily for me, politics is not so much of an obsession that it dominates my life. Yet. Thank you to you "normies" who could care less about politics but cared enough to support me.

- James and Alexandra McPhail
- Danielle Rothschild
- Idali Cincotta
- Maureen Rothschild
- Igor Stolyar
- Vincent Longobardi

And finally, to the "Friends of Linda" who got strong-armed into supporting me by my baby sister.

- Sarah Sessions
- Karin Krebs
- Garry Gibbs II

- Kathy Wood
- Jennifer Peavey

Don't worry, she can't hurt you anymore. And thank you for your support!

APPENDIX

INTRODUCTION—A SATIRE POINTED BY TRUTH

Benjamin, Liz. "Eaton Touts Brooklyn GOP 'Renaissance.'" *Capitol Confidential*. June 1, 2012. https://blog.timesunion.com/capitol/archives/133543/eaton-touts-brooklyn-gop-%E2%80%98renaissance%E2%80%99/.

Berke, Ned. "Fidler, Nelson Defeat Opponents; Does It Even Matter?" *Bklyner*. November 4, 2009. https://bklyner.com/fidler-nelson-defeat-opponents-does-it-even-matter-sheepshead-bay/.

Fairley, Matthew. "The Sharpton Scale of Buffoonery™". *Behind Enemy Lines Radio. Accessed May 6, 2022*. http://www.behindenemylinesradio.us/p/calculating-levels-of-Buffoonery-using.html.

FuturePedia. "Dr. Emmett Brown." Accessed October 3, 2021. https://backtothefuture.fandom.com/wiki/Emmett_Brown.

"Gene Berardelli—Behind Enemy Lines." *Newsmax*. Accessed May 6, 2022.https://www.newsmax.com/insiders/berardelliandgallo/id-531/.

Harper, Douglas. "'Buffoon.'" *Etymology Online*. Accessed October 4, 2021. https://www.etymonline.com/word/Buffoon.

Healey, Mark C, and Martin Appel. *Gotham Baseball: New York's All-Time Team.* Charleston, SC: The History Press, 2020.

Heil, Emily. "Host of the CPAC hot tub party: 'People were well-behaved!'". *Washington Post.* March 10, 2014. https://www.washingtonpost.com/news/reliable-source/wp/2014/03/10/host-of-the-cpac-hot-tub-party-people-were-well-behaved/.

Johnson, Samuel, and Henry John Todd. *A Dictionary of the English Language: In Which the Words Are Deduced from Their Originals; and Illustrated in Their Different Significations, by Examples from the Best Writers: Together with a History of the Language, and an English Grammar.* London, 1818.

"John Quincy Adams to Abigail Adams, 12 June 1800." *National Archives.* Accessed June 22, 2022. https://founders.archives.gov/documents/Adams/04-14-02-0151.

Leopold, Mark. "Idi Amin and the Uses of Political Buffoonery." *Yale University Press Blog.* March 23, 2021. http://blog.yalebooks.com/2021/03/23/idi-amin-and-the-uses-of-political-buffoonery/.

Lloyd, Robin. "Metric Mishap Caused Loss of NASA Orbiter." *CNN.* September 30, 2019. http://www.cnn.com/TECH/space/9909/30/mars.metric.02/.

Orwell, George. 1945. *Animal Farm.* Boston; New York: Houghton Mifflin Harcourt, Corp.

@ScottieNHughes. Hughes, Scottie Nell. "@gberardelli @BEL_Radio congratulations boys for podcast of the year at blog bash". February 26, 2015. https://twitter.com/scottienhughes/status/571154960500559872.

The Essential American Tradition: An Anthology of Striking and Significant Passages from Our National Documents, State Papers, and the Writings and Speeches of American Statesmen and Leaders from 1619 to 1924. United States: George H. Doran Company, 1925.

"Wednesday, March 18, 2015." *Talkers Magazine*. March 18, 2015. https://www.talkers.com/2015/03/18/wednesday-march-18-2015/.

Witt, Stephen. "Bklyn GOP Podcast Making National Waves." *PoliticsNY.com*. March 18, 2015. https://politicsny.com/2015/03/18/bklyn-gop-podcast-making-national-waves/.

CHAPTER 1—BLESS YOUR HEART: BUFFOONICUS SUPERSILLYOUS

Annals of Congress, House of Representatives, 16th Congress, 1st Session, pp. 1539. Accessed August 17. 2020. http://memory.loc.gov/cgi-bin/ampage?collId=llac&fileName=036/llac036.db&recNum=131.

Bartlett, John Russell. *Dictionary of Americanisms: A Glossary of Words and Phrases, Usually Regarded as Peculiar to the United States*. Hoboken, Nj: J. Wiley & Sons, 2003.

Congressman Hank Johnson. "Biography." December 11, 2012. https://hankjohnson.house.gov/about/biography.

"Disability Language Style Guide." *National Center on Disability and Journalism*. 2018. https://ncdj.org/style-guide/.

D., Sarah. "'A Learning Moment': GA. Rep. Hank Johnson Apologizes for 'Midget'-Mongering". *Twitchy*. December 13, 2012. https://twitchy.com/brettt-3136/2012/12/13/a-learning-moment-rep-hank-johnson-apologizes-for-midget-mongering/.

Fuller, Matt. "10 Most Quotable Members of Congress." *Roll Call*. August 13, 2013. https://www.rollcall.com/2013/08/13/10-most-quotable-members-of-congress-2/.

"Hank Johnson Apologizes for Using the 'M' Word in Congress." *YouTube*. Accessed August 17, 2020. https://www.youtube.com/watch?v=RAnZdRCWNDY.

Heitshusen, Valerie, and Brendan W. McGarry. *Congressional Research Service. Defense Primer: The NDAA Process (IF10515)*. January 8, 2020. https://fas.org/sgp/crs/natsec/IF10515.pdf.

Kim, Seung Min. "Johnson Apologizes for 'Midget' Analogy." *Politico*. December 13, 2012. https://www.politico.com/blogs/on-congress/2012/12/johnson-apologizes-for-midget-analogy-151942.

PROGRESSIVE CAUCUS; *Congressional Record Vol. 158, No. 161 (House of Representatives—December 13, 2012)* [Pages H6794-H6799] From the Congressional Record Online through the Government Publishing Office. https://www.congress.gov/congressional-record/2012/12/13/house-section/article/H6794-2.

Rojas, Warren. "Hank Johnson Wrassles with Change." *Roll Call*. December 13, 2012. https://www.rollcall.com/2012/12/13/hank-johnson-wrassles-with-change/.

Safire, William. *Safire's Political Dictionary*. United Kingdom, Oxford University Press, p. 89, 2008.

Schneier, Eric. "Rep. Johnson Tells 'Abnormally Small People' He Regrets Using the 'M-Word.'" *CNS News*. December 13, 2012. https://cnsnews.com/news/article/rep-johnson-tells-abnormally-small-people-he-regrets-using-m-word.

Shakespeare, William., et al. *The Complete Pelican Shakespeare*. United Kingdom: Penguin Publishing Group, 2002.

Steinberg, Brian. "MSNBC Moves Al Sharpton to Sunday Mornings." *Variety*. August 26, 2015. https://variety.com/2015/tv/news/msnbc-al-sharpton-politicsnation-sunday-1201579334/.

Stelter, Brian. "Al Sharpton Formally Named MSNBC Host." *New York Times*. August 23, 2011. https://mediadecoder.blogs.nytimes.com/2011/08/23/al-sharpton-formally-named-msnbc-host/.

US House. Committee on Armed Services. *Budget Requests from the US Pacific Command and US Forces Korea*. Hearing, May 25, 2010. H.A.S.C. No. 111–147. https://www.govinfo.gov/content/pkg/CHRG-111hhrg58295/pdf/CHRG-111hhrg58295.pdf.

US House of Representatives. "Congressional Record House Articles." December 13, 2012. https://www.congress.gov/congressional-record/2012/12/13/house-section/article/H6794-2.

Washington Free Beacon. "'Resist We Much' | Al Sharpton vs the Teleprompter #1." May 6, 2014. *YouTube*. https://www.youtube.com/watch?v=ggHWRpsMEmk.

Washington Free Beacon. "'The Thigh Military' | Al Sharpton vs the Teleprompter #2." May 14, 2014. *YouTube*. https://www.youtube.com/watch?v=VD6MTlT2Ye8.

Washington Free Beacon. "'UseTube Celebrities' | Al Sharpton vs the Teleprompter #4." January 26, 2015. *YouTube*. https://www.youtube.com/watch?v=B0Q5sE8u6ek.

"Watch Saturday Night Live Highlight: Joyride with Perot." *NBC*. April 11, 2016. https://www.nbc.com/saturday-night-live/video/joyride-with-perot/n10313.

CHAPTER 2—CHEWING UP THE SCENERY: BUFFOONICUS INCREDULOUS

Axelrod, Tal. "GOP Mocks Booker's 'Spartacus' Moment." *The Hill*. September 6, 2018. https://thehill.com/homenews/senate/405394-gop-mocks-bookers-spartacus-moment?rl=1.

Bredderman, Will. "Raucous Caucus! Golden and Eaton Collide at Brooklyn GOP Convention." *The Brooklyn Paper*. October 2, 2013. https://www.brooklynpaper.com/raucous-caucus-golden-and-eaton-collide-at-brooklyn-gop-convention/.

Brown, Lee. "VP Kamala Harris Laughs When Asked about Tragedy in Afghanistan." *New York Post*. August 23, 2021. https://nypost.com/2021/08/23/kamala-harris-laughs-when-asked-about-tragedy-in-afghanistan/.

"Booker Releases 'Confidential' Kavanaugh Documents." *The Hill*. September 6, 2018. https://thehill.com/homenews/senate/405345-booker-releases-confidential-kavanaugh-documents.

Datoc, Christian. "1992: Al Sharpton Was a Big Fan of 'Offing the Pigs,' Using 'Hate' To Achieve Racial Justice." *The Daily Caller*. July 12, 2016. https://dailycaller.com/2016/07/12/1992-al-sharpton-was-a-big-fan-of-offing-the-pigs-using-hate-to-achieve-racial-justice-video/.

Desanctis, Alexandra. "Cory Booker Melts Down, Yells at DHS Secretary Kirstjen Nielsen over Trump Comments." *National Review*. January 16, 2018. https://www.nationalreview.com/corner/cory-booker-kirstjen-nielsen-senator-angry-over-trumps-immigration-comments/.

Duhigg, Charles. "Charles Duhigg: Why Is America so Angry?" *The Atlantic*. December 10, 2018. https://www.theatlantic.com/magazine/archive/2019/01/charles-duhigg-american-anger/576424/.

"Enclosure: James McHenry to John Adams, 31 May 1800," Founders Online, *National Archives*. Accessed August 31, 2021. https://founders.archives.gov/documents/Hamilton/01-24-02-0469-0003.

"Enclosure: James McHenry to John McHenry, Junior, 20 May 1800," Founders Online, *National Archives*. Accessed August 31, 2021. https://founders.archives.gov/documents/Hamilton/01-24-02-0422-0002.

"From Alexander Hamilton to George Washington, 21 October 1799," Founders Online, *National Archives*. Accessed August 31, 2021. https://founders.archives.gov/documents/Hamilton/01-23-02-0492.

"From John Adams to Benjamin Rush, 25 January 1806," Founders Online, *National Archives*, https://founders.archives.gov/documents/Adams/99-02-02-5119.

Groth, Jeff, dir. Todd Phillips. *Joker*. 2019. Burbank, CA: Warner Bros. Pictures, 2020.

Hains, Tim. "Cory Booker: 'I Am Frankly Seething with Anger' Over Trump Comments, 'Had Tears Of Rage.'" *RealClearPolitics*. January 16, 2018. https://www.realclearpolitics.com/video/2018/01/16/cory_booker_i_am_frankly_seething_with_anger_over_s-hole_comments_had_tears_of_rage.html/.

Kogan, Rick. "Morton Downey Jr. paved the way for the angry talk show host of today." *Chicago Tribune*. August 17, 2015. https://www.chicagotribune.com/entertainment/tv/ct-morton-downey-jr-documentary-20150817-story.html.

"Letter from Alexander Hamilton, Concerning the Public Conduct and Character of John Adams, Esq. President of the United States, [24 October 1800]." Founders Online, *National Archives*. January 25, 2002. https://founders.archives.gov/documents/Hamilton/01-25-02-0110-0002.

Mayo Clinic Family Health Book 5th Edition: Completely Revised and Updated. United States: Mayo Clinic Press, 2018.

Parker, Kathleen. "Opinion: Cory Booker's 'Spartacus' Moment." *Washington Post*. September 7, 2018. https://www.washingtonpost.com/opinions/cory-bookers-spartacus-moment/2018/09/07/8c97eaee-b2f6-11e8-aed9-001309990777_story.html.

Peyser, Marc. "Takin It to the Streets." *Stanford Magazine*. Accessed June 29, 2021. https://stanfordmag.org/contents/taking-it-to-the-streets.

Raab, Scott. "The Battle of Newark, Starring Cory Booker." *Esquire*. July 16, 2008. https://www.esquire.com/news-politics/a4732/cory-booker-0708/.

"Roy Innis Pushes Al Sharpton." *Washington Post*. August 11, 1988. https://www.washingtonpost.com/archive/lifestyle/1988/08/11/

roy-innis-pushes-al-sharpton/6f39e725-6fda-4d40-b54c-d7dd4bc7f3b2/.

Salo, Jackie, Emily Jacobs, and Steven Nelson. "Kamala Harris' Response to Border Crisis a Head-Scratcher: I Haven't 'Been to Europe' Either." *New York Post.* June 8, 2021. https://nypost.com/2021/06/08/kamala-harris-dismisses-criticism-for-not-visiting-us-border/.

Schmidt, Hon. David I. "Decision—Matter of Rudiano, Et. Al., v. Eaton, Et. Al." *Scribd.* February 28, 2014. https://www.scribd.com/doc/209900475/Decision-Matter-of-Rudiano-et-al-v-Eaton-et-al?post_id=1173482469_10202374615704751.

Smith, Richard Norton. "The Surprising George Washington." *Prologue Magazine.* Spring 1994, Vol. 26, No. 1. Accessed September 1, 2021. https://www.archives.gov/publications/prologue/1994/spring/george-washington-1.html.

"The XYZ Affair and the Quasi-War with France, 1798–1800" US Department of State, Foreign Service Institute, Office of the Historian. Accessed August 31, 2021. https://history.state.gov/milestones/1784-1800/xyz.

von Spakovsky, Hans A. "Kavanaugh Hearing Day Four: Democrats Still Land No Punches." *The Heritage Foundation.* September 10, 2018. https://www.heritage.org/courts/commentary/kavanaugh-hearing-day-four-democrats-still-land-no-punches.

CHAPTER 3—CHASING THE DRAGON: BUFFOONICUS CONTORTIUS

Antenucci, Antonio, Carl Campanile, and Kate Sheehy. "Sharpton on Helping FBI: I'm Not a Rat, I'm a Cat." *New York Post.* April 8, 2014. https://nypost.com/2014/04/08/spying-on-mob-for-fbi-is-old-news-sharpton/.

"Are There Two Bryans?" *Plymouth Tribune,* Volume 3, Number 49. *Chronicling America: Historic American Newspapers.* September 8, 1904. https://chroniclingamerica.loc.gov/lccn/sn87056244/1904-09-08/ed-1/seq-1/.

Blastone, William, Andrew Goldberg, and Joseph Jesselli. "Al Sharpton's Secret Work as FBI Informant." *The Smoking Gun.* April 2, 2014. http://www.thesmokinggun.com/documents/investigation/al-sharpton-764312.

Bryan, William Jennings. *The First Battle: A Story of the Campaign of 1896. Chronicling America: Historic American Newspapers.* July 15, 1904. https://www.loc.gov/item/sn83040052/1904-07-15/ed-1/.

Cambern, Donn, dir. David S. Ward. *Major League II.* Burbank, CA 1994: Warner Bros.

Campanile, Carl, and Kate Sheehy. "Sharpton Secretly Worked as FBI Mob Informant: Report." *New York Post.* April 7, 2014. https://https://nypost.com/2014/04/07/al-sharpton-secretly-worked-as-an-fbi-mob-informant-report/.

"Elk Point, Union County, D.T. [SD]." *Union County Courier. Chronicling America: Historic American Newspapers.* July 21, 1904. https://chroniclingamerica.loc.gov/lccn/sn84022137/1904-07-21/ed-1/seq-1/.

Dickinson, Edward B. *Official Proceedings of the Democratic National Convention.* p. 226-234. "Graham on House Articles of Impeachment." December 10, 2019. https://www.lgraham.senate.gov/public/index.cfm/2019/12/graham-on-house-articles-of-impeachment.

Hartmann, Margaret. "Report Claims Al Sharpton Helped Bring Down Mobsters as an FBI Informant". *New York Magazine.* April 8, 2014. https://https://nymag.com/intelligencer/2014/04/sharpton-fbi-informant-mafia.html.

Logansport, Ind. "Wilson, Humphreys, and Co." December 14, 2011. https://archive.org/details/officialproceedi1896demo/page/n9/mode/2up?view=theater.

Maura Dowling. "Al Sharpton's 1992 off the pigs video" YouTube. Accessed February 5, 2021. https://www.youtube.com/watch?v=XpZoRwtvZmk.

McKee, Thomas Hudson. *The National Conventions and Platforms of All Political Parties, 1789 to 1904: Convention, Popular, and Electoral Vote; Also the Political Complexion of Both Houses of Congress at Each Biennial Period.* United States: Friedenwald Company, 1904.

"Notable & Quotable: Nadler against Impeachment." *The Wall Street Journal*. December 19, 2019. https://www.wsj.com/articles/notable-quotable-nadler-against-impeachment-11576713857.

"Parker and Davis It Is." *Chronicling America: Historic American Newspapers*. July 10, 1904. https://chroniclingamerica.loc.gov/lccn/sn90059523/1904-07-10/ed-1/seq-11/.

Stevenson, Frederick Boyd. "Bryan Today and Bryan To-Morrow." *Chronicling America: Historic American Newspapers*. April 28, 1907. https://chroniclingamerica.loc.gov/lccn/sn84026749/1907-04-28/ed-1/seq-47/.

"Transcript: House Manager Graham's Statement on Constitutional Law." *CNN*. January 16, 1999. https://www.cnn.com/ALLPOLITICS/stories/1999/01/16/transcripts/graham.html.

US Congress, Committee on the Judiciary. *Impeachment of William Jefferson Clinton, President of the United States*. 105th Cong. 2nd Sess., 1998. https://www.congress.gov/105/crpt/hrpt830/CRPT-105hrpt830.pdf.

Warren, Lee. "Cheering for Clothes?" *SBNation Minor League Ball*. November 30, 2013. https://www.minorleagueball.com/2013/11/30/5159958/cheering-for-clothes.

CHAPTER 4—LOST IN ALL THEIR GLORY: BUFFOONICUS OBLIVIOUS

Asma, Khalid. "Warren Releases DNA Results, Challenges Trump Over Native American Ancestry." *NPR*. October 15, 2018. https://www.npr.org/2018/10/15/657468655/warren-releases-dna-results-challenges-trump-over-native-american-ancestry.

Bell, Elvin C. "Lechery and Cowardice" August 22, 1879. https://lccn.loc.gov/sn84026918.

"Canonchet, Sprague Home, Is Burned." *New York Times*. October 12, 1909. https://www.nytimes.com/1909/10/12/archives/canonchet-sprague-home-is-burned-war-governor-in-danger-as-place-is.html.

Cilliza, Chris. "Elizabeth Warren's Native-American Heritage Reveal Was Just as Bad as You Thought It Was." *CNN*. December 7, 2018. https://www.cnn.com/2018/12/06/politics/elizabeth-warren-native-american/index.html.

Concha, Joe. "Media Embrace of Warren's 1/1,024TH Heritage an Epic Failure." *The Hill*. October 16, 2018. https://thehill.com/opinion/campaign/411633-media-embrace-of-warrens-1-1024th-heritage-an-epic-failure.

Depew, Chauncey Mitchell. *My Memories of Eighty Years*. United States, C. Scribner's Sons, 1922.

Dewberry, Sarah. "Cherokee Nation Issues Statement on Sen. Elizabeth Warren's DNA Test Results." *KJRH.com*. October 15, 2018. https://www.kjrh.com/news/local-news/cherokee-nation-issues-statement-on-sen-elizabeth-warren-s-dna-test-results.

Francke-Buta, Garance. "Is Elizabeth Warren Native American or What?" *The Atlantic*. May 20, 2012. https://www.theatlantic.com/politics/archive/2012/05/is-elizabeth-warren-native-american-or-what/257415/.

Fulani, Dr. Lenora. "The Real Al Sharpton." *BlackElectorate.com*. March 10, 2003. http://www.blackelectorate.com/articles.asp?ID=822.

Goodwin, Doris Kearns. *Team of Rivals: The Political Genius of Abraham Lincoln*. United States, Simon & Schuster, 2006.

Hod, Itay. "Sriracha Gate? Hillary Clinton Mocked Mercilessly for Hot Sauce Comment." *The Wrap*. April 18, 2016. https://www.thewrap.com/sriracha-gate-hillary-clinton-mocked-mercilessly-for-hot-sauce-comment/.

Holy Bible: English Standard Version, Morroco, Leather, Minister's Bible. Hendrickson Publishers, 2009.

Linskey, Annie, and Amy Gardner. "Elizabeth Warren Apologizes for Calling Herself Native American." *Washington Post*. February 5, 2019. https://www.washingtonpost.com/politics/elizabeth-warren-apologizes-for-calling-herself-native-american/2019/02/05/1627df76-2962-11e9-984d-9b8fba003e81_story.html.

Mayo Clinic. "Narcissistic Personality Disorder." Accessed September 4, 2021. https://www.mayoclinic.org/diseases-conditions/narcissistic-personality-disorder/symptoms-causes/syc-20366662.

Mazza, Ed. "Ted Cruz's Flimsy Excuse for His Cancun Beach Vacation Just Fell Apart." *Huffington Post*. February 22, 2021. https://www.huffpost.com/entry/ted-cruz-cancun-friend_n_60334af-4c5b66dfc101fb9e9.

McManus, Bob. "Trump Is Absolutely Right About 'Con Man' Al Sharpton." *New York Post*. July 30, 2019. https://nypost.com/2019/07/29/trump-is-absolutely-right-about-con-man-al-sharpton/

Moser, Edward P. *The White House's Unruly Neighborhood: Crime, Scandal and Intrigue in the History of Lafayette Square*. p. 17. United States, McFarland, Incorporated, Publishers, 2019.

Moya-Smith, Simon. "Elizabeth Warren's Native Ancestry Claims Never Compelled an Apology before She Ran for President. So Spare Us Now." *NBC News*. February 9, 2019. https://www.nbcnews.com/think/opinion/elizabeth-warren-s-native-ancestry-claims-never-compelled-apology-she-ncna968801.

"Mr. Conkling nervous; A Witness in the Jesse Hoyt Will Case Who Troubled Him." *New York Times*. Accessed September 7, 2021.https://www.nytimes.com/1884/03/25/archives/mr-conkling-nervous-a-witness-in-the-jesse-hoyt-will-case-who.html.

New England Historical Society. "Rhode Island's Sprague-Conkling Affair (or the 1879 Episode at Narragansett)." Accessed September 7, 2021. https://www.newenglandhistoricalsociety.com/rhode-islands-sprague-conkling-affair-1879-episode-at-narragansett/.

Nickisch, Curt. "In Mass. Senate Race, Warren on the Defensive over Native American Heritage." *NPR*. May 1, 2012. https://www.npr.org/sections/itsallpolitics/2012/05/09/151784645/in-mass-senate-race-warren-on-defense-over-native-american-heritage.

Parker, Ashley. "One Night in Cancun: Ted Cruz's Disastrous Decision to Go On Vacation during Texas Storm Crisis." *Washington Post*. February 19, 2021. https://www.washingtonpost.com/politics/ted-cruz-cancun-storm/2021/02/19/ce1dc25e-7252-11eb-93be-c10813e358a2_story.html.

Peoples, Steve, Jake Bleiberg. "'Obviously a Mistake': Cruz Returns from Cancun after Uproar." *Associated Press*. February 18, 2021. https://apnews.com/article/ted-cruz-mexico-vacation-amid-storm-b0cdc326db95bf25d93de9e877e05862.

Poor, Jeff. "Elizabeth Warren: 'I'm Proud of My Native American Heritage." *Daily Caller*. May 14, 2012. https://dailycaller.com/2012/05/14/elizabeth-warren-im-proud-of-my-native-american-heritage/.

Steinbuch, Yaron. "Elizabeth Warren Apologizes to Cherokee Nation for DNA Test." *New York Post.* February 1, 2019. https://nypost.com/2019/02/01/elizabeth-warren-apologizes-to-cherokee-nation-for-dna-test/.

US Senate. "About the Vice President | Chester Alan Arthur, 20th Vice President (1881)". Accessed September 7, 2021. https://www.senate.gov/about/officers-staff/vice-president/arthur-chester.htm.

US Senate. "Once the Senatorial Apollo—Now the Court-Jester." April 23, 1884. https://www.senate.gov/art-artifacts/historical-images/political-cartoons-caricatures/38_00349.htm.

Wolff, Wendy, ed. *Vice Presidents of the United States, 1789-1993.* United States: US Government Printing Office, 1997.

Zhang, Sarah. "The First DNA Test as Political Stunt." *The Atlantic.* October 15, 2018. https://www.theatlantic.com/science/archive/2018/10/elizabeth-warren-dna-test/572998/.

@TheRevAl (Reverend Al Sharpton). "Headed to Minneapolis to stand with the Floyd family as closing arguments are set to be made today." *Twitter.* April 19, 2021. 7:21 AM. https://twitter.com/TheRevAl/status/1384104985684635652.

CHAPTER 5—SUCCUBI AND SNOLLYGOSTERS: BUFFOONICUS PARASITOS

Alexandria Ocasio-Cortez. "About." Accessed September 23, 2021. https://ocasio-cortez.house.gov/about.

"Andrew J (Bossy) Gillis Dies; Once Called 'Bad Boy Mayor." *New York Times.* November 5, 1965. https://www.nytimes.com/1965/11/05/archives/andrew-j-bossy-gillis-dies-once-called-bad-boy-mayor-ran-in.html.

Benwell, Max. "🍎😂🎉: How Alexandria Ocasio-Cortez Beat Everyone at Twitter in Nine Tweets." *The Guardian.* February

12, 2019. https://www.theguardian.com/us-news/2019/feb/12/alexandria-ocasio-cortez-twitter-social-media.

Berggren, D. Jason. "Al Sharpton." *Southern Methodist University*. Accessed September 28, 2021. http://cphcmp.smu.edu/2004election/al-sharpton-2/.

"'Bossy' Gillis Gets Two Months' Jail Term; Newburyport Mayor Also Is Fined $545." *New York Times*. October 5, 1928. https://www.nytimes.com/1928/10/05/archives/bossy-gillis-gets-two-months-jail-term-newburyport-mayor-also-is.html.

"Bossy Gillis, Two-Fisted Mayor, May Seek Fourth Term, But He 'Ain't Saying" *Reading Eagle*. August 1, 1937. https://news.google.com/newspapers?id=1LIhAAAAIBAJ&sjid=t5sFAAAAIBAJ&pg=3573%2C120750.

Brown, Joel. "'Life in Newburyport,' One Story at a Time." *Boston.com*. October 14, 2010. http://archive.boston.com/ae/books/articles/2010/10/14/retired_teacher_doyle_uses_stories_to_recount_life_in_newburyport_1950_85/.

"City of Newburyport Massachusetts." Accessed September 27, 2021. https://www.cityofnewburyport.com.

Congress.gov. "Alexandria Ocasio-Cortez." Accessed May 17, 2022. https://www.congress.gov/member/alexandria-ocasio-cortez/O000172?q=%7B%22sponsorship%22%3A%22sponsored%22%2C%22congress%22%3A117%7D.

Congress.gov. "Alexandria Ocasio-Cortez." Accessed September 23, 2021. https://www.congress.gov/member/alexandria-ocasio-cortez/O000172.

Cox, Jeff. "Former Fed Chair Alan Greenspan thinks the Ocasio-Cortez 70% tax plan is 'a terrible idea.'" *CNBC*. January 7, 2019. https://www.cnbc.com/2019/01/07/alan-greenspan-thinks-the-ocasio-cortez-70percent-tax-plan-is-a-terrible-idea.html.

Dwyer, Colin. "From Seussian to Snollygoster, Merriam-Webster Adds Over 1,000 New Words." *NPR*. February 8, 2017. https://www.npr.org/sections/thetwo-way/2017/02/08/514074593/from-seussian-to-snollygoster-merriam-webster-adds-over-1-000-new-words.

"HEROES: In Newburyport." *Time*. January 16, 1928. http://content.time.com/time/subscriber/article/0,33009,731334,00.html.

Hicky, Louise McHenry. "Wherefore Snollygoster?" *The Georgia Review*, vol. 11, no. 1, Board of Regents of the University System of Georgia by and on Behalf of the University of Georgia and the Georgia Review, 1957, pp. 86–90, http://www.jstor.org/stable/41396150.

"In the Crossfire The Rev. Al Sharpton for president?" *CNN*. January 27, 2003. http://edition.cnn.com/2003/ALLPOLITICS/01/27/cf.opinion.al.sharpton/.

Kornacki, Steve. "2004: Sharpton, Moseley Braun Make a Run for the Nomination." *NBC News*. July 29, 2019. https://www.nbcnews.com/politics/elections/2004-sharpton-moseley-braun-make-run-nomination-n1029616.

Kurtz, Judy. "Ocasio-Cortez Attends Met Gala Wearing 'Tax the Rich' Dress." *The Hill*. September 13, 2021. https://thehill.com/blogs/in-the-know/572085-ocasio-cortez-attends-met-gala-wearing-dress-that-reads-tax-the-rich.

Lagoulis, John. "Remembering Newburyport's Bossy Gillis." *NewportburyNews.com*. May 12, 2012. https://www.newburyportnews.com/news/local_news/remembering-newburyports-bossy-gillis/article_6aff0af9-8914-5701-870c-0d87bd235e07.html.

Leirer, Bobby, and Tony Lombardo, dir. Jonathan Lynn. *The Distinguished Gentleman*. 1992; Burbank, CA: Buena Vista Pictures, 1993.

Levine, Jon, and Kathianne Boriello. "AOC's 'Tax the Rich' Dress Designer Aurora James Owes Debt in Multiple States." *New York Post*. September 18, 2021. https://nypost.com/2021/09/18/aocs-tax-the-rich-dress-designer-aurora-james-is-a-tax-deadbeat/.

McCarthy, Shawn. "Presidency Not Prize Sharpton's Pursuing." *The Globe and Mail*. March 1, 2004. https://www.theglobeandmail.com/news/world/presidency-not-prize-sharptons-pursuing/article4087763/.

Merriam-Webster. "What's a Snollygaster?" Accessed September 21, 2021. https://www.merriam-webster.com/words-at-play/whats-a-snollygoster.

Open Secrets. "Rep. "Alexandria Ocasio-Cortez—Campaign Finance Summary." Accessed September 24, 2021. https://www.opensecrets.org/members-of-congress/alexandria-ocasio-cortez/summary?cid=N00041162&cycle=2022&type=C.

Portillo, Priscilla. "Newportbury History Buffs | A friend gave me this "Bossy Gillis" piece of history......ever see one?" *Facebook*. April 24, 2021, at 10:37 PM. https://www.facebook.com/groups/28280126781/posts/10157939583626782/?comment_id=10157942851786782.

Seinfeld, Jerry. *Is This Anything?*. United States, Simon & Schuster, 2020.

Sharpton, Al. "Candidates / Al Sharpton." *CNN*. Accessed September 28, 2021. http://www.cnn.com/ELECTION/2004/special/president/candidates/sharpton.html.

"THE NATION. Peace?" *Time*. May 5, 1947. http://content.time.com/time/subscriber/article/0,33009,793626,00.html.

Warren, Susan. "Ocasio-Cortez Blasts Capitalism as an 'Irredeemable' System." *Bloomberg*. March 10, 2019. https://www.bloomberg.com/news/articles/2019-03-10/ocasio-cortez-blasts-capitalism-as-an-irredeemable-system.

Wilder, Roy. *You All Spoken Here*. Greece, University of Georgia Press, 1998.

CHAPTER 6—FOR THE CULTURE: BUFFOONICUS CELEBRITAS

Andrews, Travis M. "Alyssa Milano Weighs in on Brett Kavanaugh Allegations as #WhyIDidntReport Goes Viral." *Washington Post*. September 23, 2018. https://www.washingtonpost.com/news/arts-and-entertainment/wp/2018/09/23/alyssa-milano-weighs-in-on-brett-kavanaugh-allegations-as-whyididntreport-goes-viral/.

Berkman, Meredith. "Al Sharpton on 'Bonfire of the Vanities.'" *Entertainment Weekly*. January 18, 1991. https://ew.com/article/1991/01/18/al-sharpton-bonfire-vanities/.

"CALIFORNIA: The Battle of Hollywood." *Time*. February 14, 1944. http://content.time.com/time/subscriber/article/0,33009,885343,00.html.

Cherkasky, Catherine. "'Believe All Women'? Now That Reade Has Accused Joe Biden of Sexual Assault, Never Mind." *USA Today*. April 29, 2020. https://www.usatoday.com/story/opinion/2020/04/29/joe-biden-tara-reade-sexual-assault-allegation-me-too-column/3040158001/.

Dewey, Donald. *James Stewart*. Sphere, London. 1997.

Felton, Emmanuel. "Alyssa Milano Is Still Standing by Joe Biden Despite Criticism She Received from Other Activists." *Buzzfeed News*. April 23, 2020. https://www.buzzfeednews.com/article/emmanuelfelton/alyssa-milano-joe-biden-endorsement.

LeVanway, William, dir. Sam Wood. *A Night at the Opera*. 1935; United States: Loew's Inc. 1936.

Louszko, Ashley, Meagan Redman, and Alexa Valiente. "Rose McGowan describes alleged rape by Harvey Weinstein, her thoughts on the Hollywood 'system.'" *ABC News*. January

30, 2018. https://abcnews.go.com/Entertainment/rose-mcgowan-describes-alleged-rape-harvey-weinstein-thoughts/story?id=52684109.

McGowan, Rose. @rosemcgowan. "You are a fraud. This is about holding the media accountable. You go after Trump & Kavanaugh saying Believe Victims, you are a lie. You have always been a lie. The corrupt DNC is in on the smear job of Tara Reade, so are you. SHAME." *Twitter.* April 6, 2020, at 3:58 PM. https://twitter.com/rosemcgowan/status/1247252442812690433.

Milano, Alyssa. "Alyssa Milano On Why She Still Supports Joe Biden & How She Would Advise Him About Tara Reade Allegations—Guest Column." *Deadline.* April 29, 2020. https://deadline.com/2020/04/alyssa-milano-joe-biden-tara-reade-allegations-guest-column-1202921826/.

Pankow, Bill. *The Bonfire of the Vanities.* Directed by Brian DePalma. United States: Warner Bros. 1991.

PowerfulJRE. "Joe Rogan Experience #1525—Tim Dillon." *YouTube,* Joe Rogan Experience, 14 Aug. 2020, https://www.youtube.com/watch?v=h9XzuUXj6Gc.

Rakich, Nathaniel and Dhrumil Mehta. "How The Media Has—And Hasn't—Covered Tara Reade's Allegation." *FiveThirtyEight.* May 5, 2020. https://fivethirtyeight.com/features/how-the-media-has-and-hasnt-covered-tara-reades-allegation-against-joe-biden/.

Sbardellati, John. *J. Edgar Hoover Goes to the Movies: The FBI and the Origins of Hollywood's Cold War.* United States, Cornell University Press, 2012.

Sheffield, Gary, Jr. "Alyssa Milano Threw Herself a Joe Rogan-Envy Themed Twitter Pity Party." *OutKick.* Accessed November 9, 2021. https://www.outkick.com/alyssa-milano-threw-herself-a-joe-rogan-envy-themed-twitter-pity-party/.

Strause, Jackie. "Alyssa Milano Describes Being in the Room for Ford-Kavanaugh Hearing: 'There Was a Lot of Rage.'" *The Hollywood Reporter*. September 28, 2018. https://www.hollywoodreporter.com/news/general-news/alyssa-milano-interview-ford-kavanaugh-hearing-1147734/.

"THE CONGRESS: From Wonderland." *Time*. October 27, 1947. http://content.time.com/time/subscriber/article/0,33009,854789,00.html.

Toto, Christian. "Alyssa Milano's MeToo Hypocrisy Has Plenty of Company." *Hollywood in Toto*. April 30, 2020. https://www.hollywoodintoto.com/alyssa-milano-metoo-hypocrisy-biden-media/.

Toto, Christian. "Joe Rogan Destroys 'Activist' Alyssa Milano: Her Phone Stopped Ringing." *NewsBusters*. August 22, 2020. https://www.newsbusters.org/blogs/nb/christian-toto/2020/08/22/joe-rogan-destroys-activist-alyssa-milano-her-phone-stopped.

Tower, Samuel A. "Film Men Admit Activity by Reds; Hold It Is Foiled." *New York Times*. October 21, 1947. https://www.nytimes.com/1947/10/21/archives/film-men-admit-activity-by-reds-hold-it-is-foiled-sam-wood-lists.html.

Watts, Steven. *The Magic Kingdom: Walt Disney and the American Way of Life*. p. 240. United States, University of Missouri Press, 2013.

"Who Says Washington Is "Hollywood for Ugly People?: We Trace a Cliche Back to Its Origins." *Washington Post*. December 6, 2010. http://voices.washingtonpost.com/reliable-source/2010/12/who_says_washington_is_hollywo.html.

Wray, Meaghan. "Rose McGowan Calls Alyssa Milano a 'Fraud' for Supporting Accused Joe Biden." *Global News*. April 7, 2020. https://globalnews.ca/news/6789106/rose-mcgowan-alyssa-milano-joe-biden-fight /.

Wulfsohn, Joseph. "Biden Accuser Tara Reade Trashes Alyssa Milano for Defending Candidate." *Fox News.* April 27, 2020. https://www.foxnews.com/media/biden-accuser-tara-reade-alyssa-milano.

CHAPTER 7 – MERCENARY PENS AND MICS FOR HIRE: BUFFOONICUS AD-NEWSEAM

Abbot, Willis J. *Watching the World Go By.* With Ills. United Kingdom, John Lane The Bodley Head, 1933.

Acosta, Jim. *The Enemy of the People: A Dangerous Time to Tell the Truth in America.* United States, Harper Paperbacks, 2020.

Acosta, Jim. @Acosta. "I tried to ask the president if he would stop calling us the enemy of the people. He did not respond.". *Twitter.* June 29, 2018, at 12:58 PM. https://twitter.com/Acosta/status/1012742143948050432.

Acosta, Jim. @Acosta. "Trump in Rose Garden speech paints asylum seekers with broad brush accusing them of misleading immigration authorities at border: "These are frivolous claims."*Twitter.* May 16, 2019, at 2:44 PM. https://twitter.com/Acosta/status/1129095220409307136.

Allsop, Jon and Pete Vernon. "How the Press Covered the Last Four Years of Trump." *Columbia Journalism Review.* October 23, 2020. https://www.cjr.org/special_report/coverage-trump-presidency-2020-election.php.

"A New Comer." *Journalist.* p. 77. June 26, 1897.

Breyfogle, Todd. *Literary Imagination, Ancient and Modern: Essays in Honor of David Grene.* Chicago: University of Chicago Press, 1999.

Campbell, W. Joseph. *Getting It Wrong: Debunking the Greatest Myths in American Journalism.* California: University of California Press, 2017.

Campbell, W. Joseph. *Yellow Journalism: Puncturing the Myths, Defining the Legacies.* United Kingdom: Praeger, 2001.

Concha, Joe. "The disgrace that was the Biden press conference." *The Hill.* March 26, 2021. https://thehill.com/opinion/whitehouse/545090-the-disgrace-that-was-the-biden-press-conference.

Creelman, James. *On the Great Highway: The Wanderings and Adventures of a Special Correspondent.* United States, Lothrop Publishing Company, 1901.

Cullison, Alan and Dustin Volz. "Mueller Report Dismisses Many Steele Dossier Claims." *The Wall Street Journal.* April 19, 2019. https://www.wsj.com/articles/mueller-report-dismisses-many-steele-dossier-claims-11555710147.

Dorwart, Jeffery M. "James Creelman, the New York World and the Port Arthur Massacre." *Journalism Quarterly*, vol. 50, no. 4, Dec. 1973, p. 698, doi:10.1177/107769907305000411.

Fischer, David Hackett. *Historians' Fallacies: Toward a Logic of Historical Thought.* Taiwan: HarperCollins, 1970.

Houck, Curtis. "Does He Need a Safe Space? Acosta Loses It After Hanoi Presser, Makes False Claim About WH Press." *NewsBusters.* February 28, 2019. https://www.newsbusters.org/blogs/nb/curtis-houck/2019/02/28/does-he-need-safe-space-acosta-loses-it-after-hanoi-presser-makes.

Krauthammer, Charles. "Kidnapped by the Times." *Washington Post.* August 18, 2002. https://www.washingtonpost.com/archive/opinions/2002/08/18/kidnapped-by-the-times/e9451007-50ed-4f7a-ae90-964c3679520b/.

Levine, Jon. @LevineJonathan. "OMG! CNNs @Acosta repeatedly shouts "Mr. President, will you stop calling the press the enemy of the people" at @realDonaldTrump and is shushed by an onlooker!". *Twitter.* June 29, 2018, at 3:23 PM. https://twitter.com/LevineJonathan/status/1012775962793168898.

Miele, Frank. "Jim Acosta and the Hubris of Celebrity Journalism." *RealClearPolitics*. November 19, 2018. https://www.realclearpolitics.com/articles/2018/11/19/jim_acosta_and_the_hubris_of_celebrity_journalism.html.

Nolte, John. "Nolte: CNN's Acosta Caught Lying During Tantrum at Hanoi Press Conference." *Breitbart News*. February 28, 2019. https://www.breitbart.com/the-media/2019/02/28/nolte-cnns-acosta-caught-lying-tantrum-hanoi-press-conference/.

Quinn, Annalisa. "In 'the Enemy of the People,' CNN Reporter Recounts His Time Covering President Trump." *NPR*. June 11, 2019. https://www.npr.org/2019/06/11/731593232/in-the-enemy-of-the-people-cnn-reporter-recounts-his-time-covering-president-tru.

"Rev. Al Sharpton, the 'Refined Agitator.'" *CBS News*. May 19, 2011. http://web.archive.org/web/20110731150521/http://www.cbsnews.com/stories/2011/05/19/60minutes/main20064391.shtml.

Spiering, Charlie. @CharlieSpiering. "Full quote: 'Unfortunately legitimate asylum seekers are being displaced by those lodging frivolous claims.'" *Twitter*. May 16, 2019, at 2:49 PM. https://twitter.com/charliespiering/status/1129096540432326657.

Stiles, Andrew. "Sad Liberals: Cornel West and a Salon Columnist Attempt to Talk Through Their Obama Disillusionment." *The Washington Free Beacon*. August 25, 2014. https://freebeacon.com/blog/sad-liberals-cornel-west-and-a-salon-columnist-attempt-to-talk-through-their-obama-disillusionment/.

Sutton, Kelsey. "Trump Calls CNN 'Fake News,' as Channel Defends Its Reporting on Intelligence Briefing." *Politico*. January 11, 2017. https://www.politico.com/blogs/on-media/2017/01/trump-refusing-to-answer-question-from-cnn-reporter-you-are-fake-news-233485.

"The Port Arthur Outrages," *New York Tribune.* p. 6. December 10, 1894.

Tréguer, Pascale. "How 'Grub Street' Came to Refer to Hack Work." *World Histories.* December 23, 2017. https://wordhistories.net/2017/12/23/grub-street-hack-work/.

Wulfsohn, Joseph. "Cnn's Jim Acosta Says Media 'Neutrality' Doesn't Serve Us in the Age of Trump, Admits to 'Showboating' and 'Grandstanding.'" *Fox News.* May 28, 2019. https://www.foxnews.com/entertainment/cnn-jim-acosta-trump-media-neutrality.

Wulfsohn, Joseph. "Critics Pan Jim Acosta's New Book: He Has 'Become a Commentator, Not a Reporter.'" *Fox News.* June 13, 2019. https://www.foxnews.com/entertainment/critics-pan-jim-acostas-new-book-he-has-become-a-commentator-not-a-reporter.

CHAPTER 8 – PUSHING BEYOND THE ENVELOPE: BUFFOONICUS AMBITIOUS

Anderson, Jack, and Joseph Spear. "Jesse Jackson's Overnight Celebrity." *Washington Post.* June 23, 1987. https://www.washingtonpost.com/archive/business/1987/06/23/jesse-jacksons-overnight-celebrity/6563efcd-642e-41eb-a012-6ae06ed0342d/.

Baker, Sinéad. "Judge Tosses Out Stormy Daniels' Lawsuit to Tear up the NDA to Stop Her from Talking about Her Alleged Affair with Trump." *Business Insider.* March 8, 2019. https://www.businessinsider.com/stormy-daniels-hush-money-lawsuit-trump-tossed-2019-3.

Bever, Lindsay. "Michael Avenatti furious over "CREEPY PORN LAWYER" chyron on Fox News." *Washington Post.* September 14, 2018. https://www.washingtonpost.com/news/

reliable-source/wp/2018/09/14/creepy-porn-lawyer-michael-avenatti-lashes-out-at-tucker-carlson-fox-over-name-calling/.

Campbell, Tracy. *Book Review—Short of the Glory: The Fall and Redemption of Edward E Prichard Jr*. Lexington: University Press of Kentucky, 1998. https://academic.oup.com/jah/article-abstract/86/3/1379/689072?redirectedFrom=PDF.

Campbell, Tracy. *Short of the Glory: The Fall and Redemption of Edward F. Prichard Jr*. Lexington; University Press of Kentucky, 2010.

Cooper, Anderson. "60 Minutes Investigates Medical Gear Sold During Ebola Crisis." *60 Minutes*. May 1, 2016. https://www.cbsnews.com/news/60-minutes-investigates-medical-gear-sold-during-ebola-crisis/.

D'Agostino, Bill and Rich Noyes. "UPDATE: Porn Star Lawyer Interviewed 147 Times in 10 Weeks." *NewsBusters*. May 16, 2018. https://www.newsbusters.org/blogs/nb/bill-dagostino/2018/05/16/update-porn-star-lawyer-interviewed-147-times-10-weeks.

D'Agostino, Bill. "Update: TV News Hosted Michael Avenatti 254 Times in One Year." *NewsBusters*. April 11, 2019. https://www.newsbusters.org/blogs/nb/bill-dagostino/2019/04/11/update-tv-news-hosted-michael-avenatti-254-times-one-year.

Damron, Aryssa. "MSNBC Legal Analyst: Swetnick's Allegation Against Kavanaugh is 'Not Credible" and 'Should Go Away.'" *The Washington Free Beacon*. October 2, 2018. https://freebeacon.com/politics/msnbc-legal-analyst-swetnicks-allegation-kavanaugh-not-credible-go-away/.

Dunleavy, Jerry. "The Rise and Fall of Michael Avenatti." *Yahoo*. July 8, 2021. https://www.yahoo.com/now/rise-fall-michael-avenatti-151100273.html.

"Edward F. Prichard, Prominent in the New Deal." *New York Times.* December 25, 1984. https://www.nytimes.com/1984/12/25/obituaries/edward-f-prichard-jr-prominent-in-new-deal.html.

Farache, Emily. "Christina's Court Fight." *E! Online.* October 18, 2000. https://www.eonline.com/news/40609/christina-s-court-fight.

Feuer, Alan and Ian Urbina. "Affidavit: Client 9 and Room 871." *New York Times.* March 11, 2008. https://www.nytimes.com/2008/03/11/nyregion/11night.html.

Figgis, John Neville, Baron Acton, John Emerich Edward Dalberg Acton, Laurence, Reginald Vere. *Historical Essays & Studies ...* Edited by John Neville Figgis ... and Reginald Vere Laurence. London, 1907.

Fitzpatrick, Sarah, and Tracy Connor. "Stormy Daniels Sues Trump for Defamation over 'Con Job' Tweet." *NBC News.* May 1, 2018. https://www.nbcnews.com/news/us-news/stormy-daniels-sues-trump-defamation-over-con-job-tweet-n870171.

Fox, Emily Jane. "'I Want to Be Really F—king Clear': The Epic, Inconceivable, Totally Predictable Fall of Michael Avenatti." *Vanity Fair.* February 14, 2020. https://www.vanityfair.com/news/2020/02/epic-inconceivable-totally-predictable-fall-of-michael-avenatti.

Gould, Lewis L. Organization of American Historians. *The Journal of American History.* Vol. 86, Issue 3. December 1999.

Harwood, Richard. "Edward F. Prichard Hr., FDR Brain-Truster, Dies." *Washington Post.* December 25, 1984. https://www.washingtonpost.com/archive/local/1984/12/25/edward-f-prichard-jr-fdr-brain-truster-dies/fa050f9b-c868-487f-9b14-5da62a1c2872/.

Hedegaard, Erik. "The Entertainer." *New York Magazine.* October 7, 2004. https://nymag.com/nymetro/news/people/features/10014/.

"Hospital gowns didn't protect as promised, jury says in $454-million fraud verdict." *Los Angeles Times.* April 10, 2017. https://www.latimes.com/business/la-fi-hospital-gowns-20170410-story.html.

Kim, Seung Min and Elise Viebeck. "Key Senator Refers Avenatti and Kavanaugh Accuser to Justice Department for Criminal Inquiry." *Los Angeles Times.* October 25, 2018. https://www.latimes.com/nation/politics/la-na-pol-avenatti-swetnick-investigation-20181025-story.html.

Korecki, Natasha. "Avenatti Launches His First Political Ad." *Politico.* November 1, 2018. https://www.politico.com/story/2018/11/01/avenatti-political-ad-953758.

Luciano, Michael. "Remembering the Time Brian Stelter Told Michael Avenatti, 'I'm Taking You Seriously as a Contender' in 2020." *Mediaite.* July 8, 2021. https://www.mediaite.com/tv/remembering-the-time-brian-stelter-told-michael-avenatti-im-taking-you-seriously-as-a-contender-in-2020/.

Mangan, Dan. "Michael Avenatti Announces He Will Not Run for President in 2020." *CNBC.* December 4, 2018. https://www.cnbc.com/2018/12/04/michael-avenatti-announces-he-will-not-run-for-president-in-2020.html.

Mangan, Dan. "Michael Avenatti Found Guilty in Fraud Trial over Stormy Daniels Book Money." *CNBC.* February 4, 2022. https://www.cnbc.com/2022/02/04/verdict-reached-in-michael-avenatti-fraud-trial-over-stormy-daniels-book-money.html.

"Michael Avenatti, Stormy Daniels' Ex-Lawyer, Heads to Prison for Attempted Extortion." *NPR.* July 8, 2021. https://www.npr.org/2021/07/08/1014357602/michael-avenatti-stormy-daniels-prison-nike.

Newfield, Jack. "Rev. Vs. Rev." *New York Magazine.* January 7, 2002. https://nymag.com/nymetro/news/politics/national/2004race/5570/.

Niemietz, Brian. "Stormy Daniels' Lawyer Has Negotiated Settlements with Donald Trump and Paris Hilton." *New York Daily News*. March 7, 2018. https://www.nydailynews.com/entertainment/gossip/confidential/stormy-daniels-lawyer-sued-trump-paris-hilton-article-1.3861088.

"Spitzer Stands by 'Steamroller' Boast." *Reuters*. January 31, 2007. https://www.reuters.com/article/us-usa-politics-newyork/ny-gov-spitzer-stands-by-steamroller-boast-idUSN3119261020070131.

O'Brien, Davis, Rebecca, et. al. "Michael Avenatti Charged with Attempted Extortion from Nike, Bank Fraud." *Wall Street Journal*. March 25, 2019. https://www.wsj.com/articles/attorney-avenatti-charged-with-extortion-over-alleged-threats-to-nike-11553533952.

Ortega, Ralph R. "Sharpton Political Pot Shot At Jackson Stirs Fears of Power Struggle." *South Florida Sun-Sentinel*. June 6, 2001. https://www.sun-sentinel.com/news/fl-xpm-2001-06-21-0106200977-story.html.

"Paris Settlement a Real Gem." *Page Six*. August 23, 2007. https://pagesix.com/2007/08/23/paris-settlement-a-real-gem/.

Pearce, John. "Adversity and Atonement." *Boston Globe*. May 15, 1983.

"Prichard is Guilty of Election Fraud; Ex-New Deal Official Receives Two-Year Term—Partner Found Innocent." *New York Times*. July 15, 1949. https://www.nytimes.com/1949/07/15/archives/prichard-is-guilty-of-election-fraud-exnew-deal-official-receives.html.

Ringle, Ken. "When Pride Turns to Hubris." *Washington Post*. September 12, 1998. https://www.washingtonpost.com/archive/lifestyle/1998/09/12/when-pride-turns-to-hubris/2fc035b7-99fd-4b49-98ad-dc0f06844d39/.

Shilling, Erik. "Michael Avenatti Says His Love of Racing Could Derail His Presidential Bid." *Jalopnik*. October 31, 2018. https://jalopnik.com/michael-avenatti-says-his-love-of-racin-could-derail-hi-1830133013.

Sullivan, Kate. "Federal Judge Dismisses Stormy Daniels' Defamation Lawsuit against Trump." *CNN*. October 16, 2018. https://www.cnn.com/2018/10/15/politics/stormy-daniels-lawsuit-dismissed/index.html.

Sykes, Michael. "Michael Avenatti Arrested over Domestic Violence Allegation." *Axios*. November 14, 2018. https://www.axios.com/michael-avenatti-domestic-violence-assault-police-custody-d2f655b8-5a5a-42f9-b2db-7dd853d3d40d.html.

Taibbi, Matt. "Avenatti, Wohl and the Krassensteins Prove Political Media Is a Hucksters' Paradise." *Rolling Stone*. May 29, 2019. https://www.rollingstone.com/politics/politics-news/avenatti-wohl-krassensteins-prove-political-media-is-hucksters-paradise-839032/amp/?__twitter_impression=true.

United States Department of Justice. "Lawyer Michael Avenatti Arrested on Federal Bank Fraud and Wire Fraud Charges." March 25, 2019. https://www.justice.gov/usao-cdca/pr/lawyer-michael-avenatti-arrested-federal-bank-fraud-and-wire-fraud-charges.

CHAPTER 9—THE TIPPING POINT: BUFFOONICUS SOPHISTRIUS

Callahan, Maureen. "No One's More Entitled than a Coronavirus-Positive Celebrity in the Hamptons." *New York Post*. April 18, 2020. https://nypost.com/2020/04/18/no-ones-more-entitled-than-a-coronavirus-positive-celebrity-in-hamptons/.

Concha, Joe. "Hamptons Bicyclist Files Police Report after Verbal Confrontation with CNN's Chris Cuomo: Report." *The Hill*. April 15, 2020. https://thehill.com/homenews/media/492907-

hamptons-bicyclist-files-police-report-after-verbal-confrontation-with-cnns?rl=1.

Concha, Joe. "Trump Aide Accuses CNN's Chris Cuomo of Breaking Quarantine While COVID-19 Positive in Heated Interview." *The Hill*. October 27, 2020. https://thehill.com/homenews/media/522904-trump-aide-accuses-cnns-chris-cuomo-of-breaking-quarantine-while-covid-19?rl=1.

"Congress Member Under Wet Charge." *New York Times*. March 29, 1929. https://www.nytimes.com/1929/03/29/archives/congress-member-under-wet-charge-representative-michaelson-was.html.

Creitz, Charles. "CNN's C Hris Cuomo Was 'like a Boiling Pot' in Easter Clash over Breaking Quarantine, Cyclist Says." *Fox News*. April 24, 2020. https://www.foxnews.com/media/cnns-chris-cuomo-was-like-a-boiling-pot-in-confrontation-over-breaking-quarantine-cyclist-says.

"Customs Men Insist Dry Congressman Brought in Liquor." *New York Times*. March 30, 1929. https://www.nytimes.com/1929/03/30/archives/customs-men-insist-dry-congressman-brought-in-liquor-report-to.html.

"Dry Congressman Indicted in Capital." *New York Times*. November 20, 1929. https://www.nytimes.com/1929/11/20/archives/dry-representative-indicted-in-capital-on-liquor-charge-edward-e.html.

Ehrenhalt, Alan. "Hypocrisy Has Its Virtues." *New York Times*. February 6, 2001. https://www.nytimes.com/2001/02/06/opinion/hypocrisy-has-its-virtues.html.

"Evidence Points to Deceit by Brawley." *New York Times*. September 27, 1988. https://www.nytimes.com/1988/09/27/nyregion/evidence-points-to-deceit-by-brawley.html.

Goldman, John J. "Jury Rules Against Sharpton, Brawley Advisors." *Los Angeles Times*. July 14, 1998. https://www.latimes.com/archives/la-xpm-1998-jul-14-mn-3643-story.html.

Gold, Hannah. "The Chris Cuomo 'Fredo' Controversy, Explained." *The Cut*. August 13, 2019. https://www.thecut.com/2019/08/the-chris-cuomo-fredo-controversy-explained.html.

Grossman, Mark. *Political Corruption in America: An Encyclopedia of Scandals, Power, and Greed*. United States, Grey House Publishing, 2008.

Klein, Philip. "Gingrich Flunks the Al Sharpton test." *Washington Examiner*. November 22, 2011. https://www.washingtonexaminer.com/gingrich-flunks-the-al-sharpton-test.

Kratz, Jessie. "First Lady of Law: Mabel Walker Willebrandt." *National Archives*. March 18, 2021. https://prologue.blogs.archives.gov/2021/03/18/first-lady-of-law-mabel-walker-willebrandt/.

"Legislating the Liquor Law—Prohibition and the House." US House of Representatives—History, Art & Archives. August 13, 2019. https://history.house.gov/Blog/2019/August/8-13-Volstead/.

Okrent, Daniel. *Last Call: The Rise and Fall of Prohibition*. p. 324. United Kingdom, Scribner, 2010.

"PROHIBITION: Drinks for Drys." *Time*. April 8, 1929. http://content.time.com/time/subscriber/article/0,33009,732223-1,00.html.

"PROHIBITION: Fall Guy." *Time*. November 4, 1929. http://content.time.com/time/subscriber/article/0,33009,787492,00.html.

Raymond, Adam K. "Chris Cuomo Airs Moment He Could 'Finally Emerge' From Basement, a Week After Leaving Basement." *New York Magazine*. April 21, 2020. https://nymag.com/

intelligencer/2020/04/chris-cuomo-airs-dramatic-and-dramatized-basement-exit.html.

"Sharpton Admits Rape Claim Wasn't Firsthand." *Chicago Tribune.* February 10, 1998. https://www.chicagotribune.com/news/ct-xpm-1998-02-10-9802100281-story.html.

"Silence Dogood, No. 9, 23 July 1722," Founders Online, *National Archives.* Accessed September 15, 2021. https://founders.archives.gov/documents/Franklin/01-01-02-0016_.

Tapp, Tom. "CNN's Chris Cuomo Rips Donald Trump's Choreographed Return to White House: 'What a Bunch of Bullsh*t.'" *Deadline.* October 5, 2020. https://deadline.com/2020/10/cnn-chris-cuomo-rips-donald-trumps-return-to-white-house-bullshit-1234591942/.

US v. Denison, 47 F.2d 433 (D.C. Cir. 1931)

US House of Representatives. "Edward Everett Denison." Accessed September 15, 2021. https://history.house.gov/Collection/Detail/30338.

Wells, Kristina. "Sharpton Pays $88,000 in Damages Owed from Brawley Trial." *Times Herald-Record.* June 16, 2001. https://www.recordonline.com/article/20010616/NEWS/306169997.

Wilkinson, Alissa. "CNN's Chris Cuomo Said 'Fredo' Is Like 'the N-Word' for Italians. It's … Not." *Vox.* August 13, 2019. https://www.vox.com/culture/2019/8/13/20804039/chris-cuomo-fredo-godfather.

Willebrandt, Mabel Walker. "The Inside of Prohibition Chapter 11—Are Congressmen Above the Law? Bootleggers in the Capitol. Congressmen Who Sneer at Law." Hypocrisy Prohibition's Enemy. Congressional Junkets." *New York Times.* August 18, 1929. https://www.nytimes.com/1929/08/18/archives/the-inside-of-prohibition-in-this-article-mrs-willebrandt-describes.html.

CHAPTER 10 —TRIGGER WARNING: BUFFOONICUS EXTREMIS

Allen, William Cicero. *History of Halifax County*. 1917. United States, Cornhill Company, 1918.

" Article about Jesse Bynum and Robert Potter Feud in in 1825 Halifax." *Fayetteville Semi-Weekly Observer*. April 4, 1859. https://www.newspapers.com/clip/792282/article-about-jesse-bynum-and-robert/.

Bailey, Julius. *Racism, Hypocrisy, and Bad Faith: A Moral Challenge to the America I Love*. Peterborough, Ontario; Broadview Press, 2020.

Benson, Guy. "Audio: Al Sharpton's Thoughts on 'Chinamen' and 'Homos.'" *Town Hall*. March 14, 2012. https://townhall.com/tipsheet/guybenson/2012/03/14/audio-al-sharptons-thoughts-on-chinamen-and-homos-n667644.

Daughterty, Alane K., Ph.D. "Why You Freak Out." *Psychology Today*. January 23, 2020. https://www.psychologytoday.com/us/blog/healing-stress-the-inside-out/202001/why-you-freak-out/.

Dowling, Maura. "Al Sharpton's 1992 off the pigs video." *YouTube*. March 19, 2016. https://www.youtube.com/watch?v=XpZoRwtvZmk.

Ehrlich, Jamie. "Maxine Waters Encourages Supporters to Harass Trump Administration Officials." *CNN*. June 25, 2018. https://www.cnn.com/2018/06/25/politics/maxine-waters-trump-officials/index.html.

Fischer, Ernest G. *Robert Potter: Founder of the Texas Navy*. 1975. United States, Pelican Publishing Company, 1976.

Jacobs, Emily. "Rep. Maxine Waters denies encouraging violence against Republicans." *New York Post*. February 8, 2021. https://nypost.com/2021/02/08/maxine-waters-denies-encouraging-violence-against-republicans/

Journal of the House of Commons. "Disciplinary Actions by the General Assembly Against Members of the House or Senate." 1834, pp. 223-224. 231, 233-234 (December 29, 1834; January 1-2, 1835); *Dictionary of North Carolina Biography*, Vol. V., p. 133; North Carolina Legislature. http://web.archive.org/web/20180423024708/https://www.ncleg.net/library/Documents/DisciplinaryActionsAgainstMembers.pdf.

Joyella, Mark. "Rev. Al Sharpton No Longer Calls People "Punk F*ggots" But New Documentary Trailer Shows He Did." *Mediaite*. December 16, 2010. https://www.mediaite.com/tv/rev-al-sharpton-no-longer-calls-people-%E2%80%9Cpunkfggots%E2%80%9D-but-new-documentary-trailer-shows-he-did/.

Manegold, Catherine S. "Sometimes the Order of the Day Is Just Maintaining Order." *New York Times*. July 30, 1994. https://www.nytimes.com/1994/07/30/us/sometimes-the-order-of-the-day-is-just-maintaining-order.html.

Miranda, Lin-Manuel, Alex Lacamoire, and Ron. Chernow. 2016. *Hamilton: An American Musical*. Los Angeles, CA: Warner/Chappell.

Perkins, Joseph. "Maxine Waters's Long History of Reckless Rhetoric." *Wall Street Journal*. April 23, 2021. https://www.wsj.com/articles/maxine-waters-long-history-of-reckless-rhetoric-11619213954.

Powe, Alicia. "Al Sharpton: 'Homos', 'Chinamen', the 'N' Word." *YouTube*. April 30, 2014. https://www.youtube.com/watch?v=4ltjowC37AM.

Storyful Viral. "Protesters Vandalize Democratic Party Headquarters in Portland, Oregon." *YouTube*. January 21, 2021. https://www.youtube.com/watch?v=hpxHPGM-nos.

Texas State Library and Archives Commission. "Robert Potter, December 1, 1835." Accessed October 8, 2021. https://www.tsl.texas.gov/exhibits/navy/rob_potter_dec1_1835_1.html.

United States House of Representatives: History, Art & Archives. "A Proper Symbol of Office." December 4, 2017. https://history.house.gov/Blog/Detail/15032450168.

US House of Representatives, Office of the Clerk. "Artifacts of the House Chamber." Accessed October 12, 2021. https://archive.ph/20120707134652/http://artandhistory.house.gov/art_artifacts/virtual_tours/splendid_hall/artifacts.aspx.

Wallace, Carolyn A. "Potter, Robert." *NCPedia*. Accessed October 8, 2021. https://www.ncpedia.org/biography/potter-robert.

Wheeler, John Hill. *Historical Sketches of North Carolina: From 1584 to 1851, Compiled from Original Records, Official Documents and Traditional Statements; with Biographical Sketches of Her Distinguished Statemen, Jurists, Lawyers, Soldiers, Divines, Etc.*, United States, Lippincott, Grambo and Company, 1851.

Williamson, Florence, et. al. *1776*. 1972. Burbank, CA: Columbia Pictures, 1973.

CHAPTER 11—THE WRETCHED REFUSE: BUFFOONICUS DETESTICUS

Babcock, Laurel, and Rich Calder. "Ex-head of Bronx GOP Admits Taking Bribe, but Spreads Blame." *New York Post*. November 12, 2013. https://nypost.com/2013/11/12/ex-head-of-bronx-gop-admits-taking-bribe-but-spreads-blame/.

Baragona, Justin. "CNN Probes News That Chris Cuomo Dug for Dirt on Bro's Foes." *Daily Beast*. November 29, 2021. https://www.thedailybeast.com/chris-cuomo-leaned-on-media-sources-to-dig-up-dirt-on-brothers-accusers.

Barron, James. "Fossella Admits He Had an Extramarital Affair." *New York Times.* May 9, 2008. https://www.nytimes.com/2008/05/09/nyregion/09fossella.html.

Berdzik, Caroline J., Jonathan L. Berkowitz, and Lisa M. Robinson. "New York State Department of Health Releases Advisory Prohibiting Nursing Homes From Denying Admission Due to Coronavirus." *Goldberg Segalla.* March 27, 2020. https://www.goldbergsegalla.com/news-and-knowledge/knowledge/nys-health-dept-releases-coronavirus-advisory.

Bierce, Ambrose. *Black Beetles in Amber.* Germany; Outlook Verlag, 2019.

Carras, Christi. "Gov. Andrew Cuomo Approves of People Who Identify as 'Cuomosexuals.'" *Los Angeles Times.* April 28, 2020. https://www.latimes.com/entertainment-arts/story/2020-04-28/andrew-cuomo-sexual-ellen-degeneres-youtube.

Carrega, Christina. "Brooklyn Political Candidate Admits to Viewing 20 Images of Child Porn: Prosecutors." *New York Daily News.* May 22, 2015. https://www.nydailynews.com/new-york/nyc-crime/bklyn-politico-busted-child-porn-prosecutors-article-1.2232386.

Casey, Nicholas. "William Boyland Jr., Ex-New York Assemblyman, Gets 14-Year Sentence for Corruption." *New York Times.* September 17, 2015. https://www.nytimes.com/2015/09/18/nyregion/william-boyland-jr-ex-brooklyn-assemblyman-sentenced-to-14-years-in-corruption-case.html.

Cohen, Richard. "A Mockery of Black Studies." *Washington Post.* May 21, 1993. https://www.washingtonpost.com/archive/opinions/1993/05/21/a-mockery-of-black-studies/2d0baa65-0df0-46db-9eb8-0953b9428935/.

Cole, Devan. "Cuomo Defends COVID Poster That Doesn't Mention New York's Pandemic Death Toll." *CNN.* July 16,

2020. https://www.cnn.com/2020/07/16/politics/andrew-cuomo-coronavirus-poster-new-york-cnntv/index.html.

Concha, Joe. "Trump Aide Accuses CNN's Chris Cuomo of Breaking Quarantine While COVID-19 Positive in Heated Interview." *The Hill*. October 27, 2020. https://thehill.com/homenews/media/522904-trump-aide-accuses-cnns-chris-cuomo-of-breaking-quarantine-while-covid-19?rl=1.

Craig, Susan, William K. Rashbaum, and Thomas Kaplan. "Cuomo's Office Hobbled Ethics Inquiries by Moreland Commission." *New York Times*. July 23, 2014. https://www.nytimes.com/2014/07/23/nyregion/governor-andrew-cuomo-and-the-short-life-of-the-moreland-commission.html.

"Cuomo on Moreland Tampering: It's My Commission." *Crain's New York*. April 24, 2014. http://web.archive.org/web/20180922173800/https://www.crainsnewyork.com/article/20140424/BLOGS04/140429924/cuomo-on-moreland-tampering-it-s-my-commission.

Dante. "All Time Spin Zone: Andrew Cuomo Defends Himself Against Allegations Claiming, 'I'm Not A Pervert, I'm Just Italian.'" *Barstool Sports*. August 10, 2021. https://www.barstoolsports.com/blog/3377826/all-time-spin-zone-andrew-cuomo-defends-himself-against-allegations-claiming-im-not-a-pervert-im-just-italian.

Dowd, Maureen. "Keeping It Rielle." *New York Times*. August 9, 2008. https://www.nytimes.com/2008/08/10/opinion/10dowd.html.

Elliott, Russell R., and Rowley, William D. *History of Nevada*. United States, University of Nebraska Press, 1987.

Gee, Marcus. "Rob Ford's Case Illustrates When Ignorance Is No Excuse." *The Globe and Mail*. January 7, 2013. https://www.theglobeandmail.com/news/toronto/rob-fords-case-illustrates-when-ignorance-is-no-excuse/article7028178/.

Gladwell, Malcolm. "Pataki Defeats CUOMO In Race Called at the Wire." *Washington Post.* November 9, 1994. https://www.washingtonpost.com/archive/politics/1994/11/09/pataki-defeats-cuomo-in-race-called-at-the-wire/9a8b0742-cf14-4018-9977-410ebc77af71/.

Goodman, J. David, Alexandra Alter, Rachel Abrams, and Luis Ferré-Sadurní. "Cuomo Set to Receive $5.1 Million From Pandemic Book Deal." *New York Times.* May 17, 2021. https://www.nytimes.com/2021/05/17/nyregion/cuomo-tax-returns-pandemic-book.html.

Gordon, John Steele. "30 Years Ago: Gary Hart's Monkey Business, and How a Candidate Got Caught." *American Heritage.* Accessed December 9, 2021. https://www.americanheritage.com/node/132685.

Hakim, Danny, and Jeremy W. Peters. "Under Fire, Paterson Ends His Campaign for Governor." *New York Times.* February 26, 2010. https://www.nytimes.com/2010/02/27/nyregion/27paterson.html.

Jewish Journal. "Sharpton and the Riots 20 Years Later." August 22, 2011. https://jewishjournal.com/commentary/opinion/95266/.

Kampeas, Ron. "Al Sharpton Admits to Using 'Cheap' Rhetoric about Jews." *The Times of Israel.* Accessed December 8, 2021. https://www.timesofisrael.com/al-sharpton-admits-to-using-cheap-rhetoric-about-jews/.

Kantor, Jodi, and Michael Gold. "Roberta Kaplan, Who Aided Cuomo, Resigns from Time's Up." *New York Times.* August 26, 2021. https://www.nytimes.com/2021/08/09/nyregion/roberta-kaplan-times-up-cuomo.html.

Keraghosian, Greg. "How Notorious Tycoon William Sharon Left Sf's Children a Still-Popular Landmark." *SFGate.* May 23, 2021. https://www.sfgate.com/sfhistory/article/William-Sharon-golden-gate-park-landmarks-16188509.php.

Lilley, William III. "Chapter 6—'Mr. Sharon and Lady'". Accessed December 5, 2021. https://newlands.stanford.edu/6-mr-sharon-and-lady/.

Madhani, Aamer. "Judge Refuses to Reduce Blagojevich's 14-Year Sentence." *USA Today.* August 9, 2016. https://www.usatoday.com/story/news/2016/08/09/ex-illinois-gov-blagojevich-resentenced-14-years-prison/88445594/.

Makley, Michael J. *The Infamous King Of The Comstock: William Sharon And The Gilded Age In The West.* United States, University of Nevada Press, 2006.

Mandel, Seth. "Al Sharpton Is Not a Lifelong Fighter for Justice." *Washington Post.* August 1, 2019. https://www.washingtonpost.com/outlook/2019/08/01/al-sharpton-is-not-lifelong-fighter-justice/.

Mathis-Lilley, Ben. "Inspiring: This Staten Island Politician Revived His Career After a DUI Revealed His Secret Second Family." *Slate.* November 3, 2021. https://slate.com/news-and-politics/2021/11/vito-fossella-political-comeback-secret-family-revelations.html.

McKinley, Jesse. "Cuomo Accepts Some Blame in Nursing Home Scandal but Denies Cover-Up." *New York Times.* February 15, 2021. https://www.nytimes.com/2021/02/15/nyregion/cuomo-nursing-homes.html.

McLaughlin, Mark. "William Sharon, King of the Comstock: Part I." *Tahoe Weekly.* July 18, 2018. https://web.archive.org/web/20200203192111/https://thetahoeweekly.com/2018/07/william-sharon-king-of-the-comstock-part-i/.

McManus, Bob. "Andrew Cuomo Managed to Kill Grandma—And New York's Economy Too." *New York Post.* May 25, 2020. https://nypost.com/2020/05/25/andrew-cuomo-managed-to-kill-grandma-and-new-yorks-economy/.

Milligan, Susan. "How Coronavirus Made Andrew Cuomo America's Governor." *US News & World Report*. March 23, 2020. https://www.usnews.com/news/health-news/articles/2020-03-23/how-coronavirus-made-andrew-cuomo-americas-governor.

Miranda, Leticia. "Cuomo Obscura: Shady Moments During New York's 'Most Transparent' Administration." *ProPublica*. March 6, 2015. https://www.propublica.org/article/cuomo-shady-moments-during-new-yorks-most-transparent-administration.

Murphy, Mary. "9 Minutes That Triggered the Crown Heights Riots 30 Years Ago." *WPIX News*. August 19, 2021. https://pix11.com/news/local-news/brooklyn/crown-heights-riots-30-years-later-august-2021/.

Niemietz, Brian. "Gov. Cuomo Says His Dating Life Still at 'Phase Zero' and Won't Reopen Anytime Soon." *New York Daily News*. July 14, 2020. https://www.nydailynews.com/snyde/ny-governor-andrew-cuomo-dating-jimmy-fallon-20200714-y55uuqzf6jbold4myzidliprgy-story.html.

Pillifant, Reid and Azi Paybarah. "F.B.I.: Boyland Took Bribes to Pay Lawyers Defending Him from Charges That He Took Bribes." *Politico*. November 29, 2014. https://www.politico.com/states/new-york/albany/story/2011/11/fbi-boyland-took-bribes-to-pay-lawyers-defending-him-from-charges-that-he-took-bribes-000000.

quesondriac. "politically radioactive." February 24, 2015. https://www.urbandictionary.com/define.php?term=politically%20radioactive.

Schwartz, Brian. "More Details Emerge on How Fired Gay Rights Group Chief Alphonso David Advised Cuomo's Team during Scandals." *CNBC*. November 30, 2021. https://www.cnbc.com/2021/11/30/alphonso-david-gave-extensive-scandal-advice-to-cuomo-advisors-records.html.

"Sharpton Stirs Tempest in Israel." Chicago Tribune. September 18, 1991. https://www.chicagotribune.com/news/ct-xpm-1991-09-18-9103100901-story.html.

State of New York, Officer of the Attorney General. "Attorney General James Releases Report on Nursing Homes' Response to COVID-19." January 28, 2021. https://ag.ny.gov/press-release/2021/attorney-general-james-releases-report-nursing-homes-response-covid-19.

State of New York, Office of the Attorney General. "Report of Investigation into Allegations of Sexual Harassment by Governor Andrew Cuomo." August 3, 2021. https://ag.ny.gov/sites/default/files/2021.08.03_nyag_-_investigative_report.pdf.

"The Moreland Commission To Investigate Public Corruption." The State of New York. Accessed December 6, 2021. https://publiccorruption.moreland.ny.gov/.

Time's Up. "About." Accessed December 8, 2021. https://timesupnow.org/about/.

Wayt, Theo. "Facebook Staffer Secretly Advised Andrew Cuomo's Team to 'Victim Shame' Accuser." New York Post. December 1, 2021. https://nypost.com/2021/12/01/facebook-staffer-advised-andrew-cuomos-team-to-victim-shame-accuser/.

SO, WHAT DID WE LEARN?

Baer, John. "The Phenomenon of Trump Rallies." *PennLive.com*. December 12, 2019. https://www.pennlive.com/news/2019/12/the-phenomenon-of-trump-rallies-john-baer.html.

Baker, Peter, and Eileen Sullivan. "Trump Publicly Urges China to Investigate the Bidens." *New York Times*. October 3, 2019. https://www.nytimes.com/2019/10/03/us/politics/trump-china-bidens.html.

Blake, Aaron. "The 'Participation Trophy' Generation." *Washington Post*. August 20, 2014. https://www.washingtonpost.

com/news/the-fix/wp/2014/08/20/meet-the-participation-trophy-generation/.

Borger, Gloria. "Republicans Try a New Excuse to Defend Trump: It's Just a Joke." *CNN.* October 7, 2019. https://www.cnn.com/2019/10/07/politics/donald-trump-joking-gloria-borger/index.html.

Cohen, Marshall. "Trump Says He Joked about Wanting Russian Help in 2016. The Facts Tell a Different Story." *CNN.* March 5, 2019. https://www.cnn.com/2019/03/05/politics/trump-emails-joke/index.html.

Durvasula, Ramani, Ph.D. "The Delusion of Meritocracy and the Culture of Entitlement." *Psychology Today.* March 21, 2019. https://www.psychologytoday.com/us/blog/guide-better-relationships/201903/the-delusion-meritocracy-and-the-culture-entitlement.

Ekins, Emily. "65% of Americans Say Millennials Are 'Entitled,' 58% of Millennials Agree." *Reason.* August 19, 2014. https://reason.com/2014/08/19/65-of-americans-say-millennials-are-enti/.

Fay, Bill. "Economic Demographics of Democrats & Liberals—Politics & Debt." *Debt.org.* Accessed December 11, 2021. https://www.debt.org/faqs/americans-in-debt/economic-demographics-democrats/.

Friedman, Uri. "Here's What Trump Actually Achieved with North Korea." *The Atlantic.* June 19, 2018. https://www.theatlantic.com/international/archive/2018/06/trump-kim-korea-success/563012/.

Goodwin, Michael. "Trump Talks about Putin, Mocking Merkel and More at Mar-a-Lago." *New York Post.* February 22, 2022. https://nypost.com/2022/02/22/trump-talks-threatening-putin-mocking-merkel-at-mar-a-lago/.

Hopf, G. Michael. *Those Who Remain: A Postapocalyptic Novel*. United States, CreateSpace Independent Publishing Platform, 2016.

Ingram, Mathew. "The 140-Character President". *Columbia Journalism Review*. Accessed December 9, 2021. https://www.cjr.org/special_report/trump-twitter-tweets-president.php.

Jenkins, Ryan. "Top 8 Millennial Shortcomings and How to Overcome Them." *Inc.com*. June 15, 2016. https://www.inc.com/ryan-jenkins/top-8-millennial-shortcomings-and-how-to-overcome-them.html.

Jones, Susan. "Rep. Comer: Dems Are Making Trump the Issue, When Biden's Been in Office for Almost 1 Year." *CNSNews.com*. December 10, 2021. https://cnsnews.com/index.php/article/washington/susan-jones/rep-comer-dems-are-making-trump-issue-when-bidens-been-office-almost.

Killough, Ashley. "Jeb Bush's Doomed Campaign." *CNN*. February 22, 2016. https://www.cnn.com/2016/02/21/politics/jeb-bushs-doomed-campaign/index.html.

Leopold, Mark. "Idi Amin and the Uses of Political Buffoonery." Yale University Press Blog. March 23, 2021. http://blog.yalebooks.com/2021/03/23/idi-amin-and-the-uses-of-political-Buffoonery/.

Mansfield, Harvey C., and Machiavelli, Niccolò. *Discourses on Livy*. United States, University of Chicago Press, 2009.

Matthews, Robert. "North Korea Crisis: Is There Method in Trump's Madness?" *The National News* (UAE). August 19, 2017. https://www.thenationalnews.com/uae/science/north-korea-crisis-is-there-method-in-trump-s-madness-1.621008.

MIlbank, Dana. "Don't Get Distracted by Trump's 'Dead Cats.'" *Washington Post*. January 25, 2017. https://www.washingtonpost.com/opinions/2017/01/25/e59a8ab6-e34a-11e6-ba11-63c4b-4fb5a63_story.html.

Moomaw, Graham. "After Crushing Loss, 'Gimmicky' Anti-trump Strategy Draws Criticism from VA. Democrats." *Virginia Mercury*. November 5, 2021. https://www.virginiamercury.com/2021/11/05/after-crushing-loss-gimmicky-anti-trump-strategy-draws-criticism-from-va-democrats/.

Mounk, Yascha. "Stop Underestimating Donald Trump." *Slate*. January 12, 2017. https://slate.com/news-and-politics/2017/01/stop-underestimating-donald-trump.html.

Nixon, Richard. *RN: The Memoirs of Richard Nixon*. United Kingdom, Simon & Schuster, 2013.

Reed, Lawrence W. "Why Limit Government?" *The Heritage Foundation*. June 21, 2004. https://www.heritage.org/political-process/report/why-limit-government.

Singer, Emily. "11 Times Trump's Offensive Comments Were 'Just a Joke.'" *American Independent*. June 22, 2020. https://americanindependent.com/donald-trump-jokes-offensive-comments-coronavirus-testing-russia-isis-white-house/.

Smith, Allan. "The White House Has a Favorite Excuse to Explain Away Some of Trump's Most Controversial Statements." *Business Insider*. February 6, 2018. https://www.businessinsider.com/trump-joking-excuse-democrats-treason-2018-2

Strauss, William., Howe, Neil. *The Fourth Turning: What the Cycles of History Tell Us About America's Next Rendezvous with Destiny*. United States: Crown, 2009.

Umeogu, Bonachristus. "Source Credibility: A Philosophical Analysis." *Open Journal of Philosophy*, 2012, Vol. 2, No. 2. p. 112-115. https://www.scirp.org/html/19184.html.

Volokh, Eugene. "Government Is Not Reason, It Is Not Eloquence—It Is Force." *The Volokh Conspiracy*. April 14, 2010. https://volokh.com/2010/04/14/government-is-not-reason-it-is-not-eloquence-it-is-force/.

Wilson, Reid. "Increasingly Active Younger Voters Liberalize Us Electorate." *The Hill*. May 15, 2021. https://thehill.com/homenews/campaign/553634-increasingly-active-younger-voters-liberalize-us-electorate.

Zitek, Emily. "Entitled People—What to Expect and How to Deal With Them." *SPSP.org*. May 15, 2019. https://www.spsp.org/news-center/blog/zitek-entitlement.

www.ingramcontent.com/pod-product-compliance
Lightning Source LLC
LaVergne TN
LVHW011948060526
838201LV00061B/4247